W9-AVE-746

BASTARD
KEYNESIANISM

Recent Titles in

Contributions in Economics and Economic History

BASTARD KEYNESIANISM

The Evolution of Economic Thinking and Policymaking since World War II

Lynn Turgeon

Contributions in Economics and Economic History, Number 180
David O. Whitten, Series Adviser

Greenwood Press
Westport, Connecticut • London

Library of Congress Cataloging-in-Publication Data

Turgeon, Lynn, 1920—
    Bastard Keynesianism : the evolution of economic thinking and
policymaking since World War II / Lynn Turgeon.
        p. cm. — (Contributions in economics and economic history,
ISSN 0084-9235 ; no. 180)
    Includes bibliographical references and index.
    ISBN 0-313-30024-0 (alk. paper)
    1. Keynesian economics. 2. United States—Economic policy.
    3. United States—Economic conditions—1945– I. Title.
    II. Series.
    HB99.7.T837 1996
    330.15′6—dc20   96-3641

British Library Cataloguing in Publication Data is available.

Library of Congress Catalog Card Number: 96-3641
ISBN: 0-313-30024-0
ISSN: 0084-9235

First published in 1996

Greenwood Press, 88 Post Road West, Westport, CT 06881
An imprint of Greenwood Publishing Group, Inc.

Printed in the United States of America

The paper used in this book complies with the
Permanent Paper Standard issued by the National
Information Standards Organization (Z39.48-1984).

10 9 8 7 6 5 4 3 2 1

Contents

Preface

What does one do with the retirement years? Some of us have a difficult time with enforced retirement, which discriminates against senior citizens. Thus, when Robert Sobel of Hofstra's New College suggested that I might like to teach a single course there in the spring of 1992, I jumped at the opportunity. This gave me time to digest some of the material I have been teaching at the Economic Principles level for more than three decades. I had earlier tried to do the same for Soviet students at Moscow State University on a Fulbright Lectureship in the Fall of 1978. This eventually resulted in the publication of *The Advanced Capitalist System* (1980), which was largely ignored at the time. Presumably, the budding supply-side economics was then the wave of the future. My conclusion that Japan and West Germany represented the two weak links in the advanced capitalist system (because of their weaker Keynesian or non-monetarist influence) seemed incredible at the time, although it was more believable by 1995.[1] Nevertheless Joan Robinson, who worked with Keynes on *The General Theory of Employment, Interest and Money*, did read it at the urging of a former student, Morty Schapiro, then at Williams College, where Robinson spent a quarter in the early 1980s. After she had gotten into it, she reportedly exclaimed, "Why he's a Keynesian!"

Robinson was the illustrious British economist who collaborated with Richard Kahn (who is given credit for inventing the "multiplier") and Keynes at Cambridge in developing the ideas that were presented as *The General Theory of Employment, Interest and Money* in 1936. As one of the truly great global economists of the twentieth century, she merited a Nobel Prize in economics, which her gender prevented her from receiving, as was conceded after her death by Paul Samuelson, the first recipient of this honor.

Presumably Robinson was differentiating my work from the "Bastard Keynesians" whom she frequently berated. At least I would like to think that this was the case. At the outset, however, it must be admitted that there were stages in Lord Keynes's life when his own ideas were clearly affected and modified by the economic environment in which he wrote. The unique nature of the British stagnation and underutilization of its potential in the 1920s no doubt gave him a head start in eventually becoming a believer in "secular stagnation," as outlined by his U.S. disciple, Alvin Hansen. The belief that the slowdown in population growth was a factor in explaining the secular stagnation of the 1930s no doubt forced him later to abandon his neo-Malthusian or antinatalist position on population in the 1920s. And the full employment brought about by World War II forced him to question some of his earlier autarkic and neomercantilist positions in order to become one of the two leading architects behind the postwar monetary institutions coming out of Bretton Woods, which were designed to lead to a postwar renaissance of international trade.

It is the Keynes of the *General Theory* as modified by his wartime and postwar positions that I have labeled "Classical Keynesian," which is very different from the Bastard Keynesianism that has been practiced by postwar economists who consider themselves "Keynesian." These latter economists have been "Military Keynesians" or "demand managers" as well as "Commercial Keynesians," to use a term coined by Robert Lekachman to describe economists who are always willing to stimulate the economy by cutting tax rates rather than by increasing government expenditures. When demand management seemed to be getting into trouble in the 1970s, as reflected in the so-called crisis in the Phillips curve, emphasis shifted back again to Commercial Keynesianism or what eventually came to be better known as "supply-side economics." In retrospect, we can see that there were certain commonalities between the Kennedy-Johnson and Reagan years since the economic policies of both administrations represented an amalgam of these two principal postwar strands of Bastard Keynesianism.

Hofstra University turned out to be an ideal location for studying postwar presidential economic policy. Beginning in 1982, the Hofstra Cultural Center organized a series of outstanding Presidential Conferences starting with one on Franklin Delano Roosevelt and working its way forward to the Reagan Conference in April 1993.[2] The conferences have turned out to resemble class reunions, with most of the principal actors in the various administrations attending. What has transpired is a spirited dialogue between the policymakers and their critics. In my case, I have had the opportunity to confront and question such important postwar economic policymakers as Leon Keyserling, Raymond Salnier, Walter Heller, Gardner Ackley, Paul McCracken, Herbert Stein, Charles Schultze, Martin Anderson, and Murray Weidenbaum.

Important contributions to this book were performed by three of our New College students, who did research papers using Hofstra's fine library: Paul Gallagher (NSC-68); Scott Kaufman (Carter's four-year military spending plan); and Sandra Perez (Export-Import Bank). Others who have been especially kind enough to read the manuscript, but do not necessarily agree with the substance or conclusions, were Locke Anderson (who went through the whole manuscript with great editorial skill), Timothy Canova, Paul Davidson, Jeff Frieden, Sean Gervasi, Morty Greenhouse, Robert Horn, Gonzalo Lopez, Gottfried Paasche, Dorothy Rosenberg, Barkley Rosser, A.J. Sobczak, Bob Sobel, Lottie Tartell, Alan Weiss, Murray Yanowitch, and June Zaccone.

Introduction

The economics of World War II represented a thundering validation of Keynesian economics, as expounded in Keynes's *General Theory*. It is no exaggeration to suggest that virtually all major economists had been converted by the brilliant successes of the U.S. economy during the war to the economics of the *General Theory*, as opposed to Keynes's earlier *Treatise on Money* or the *Economic Consequences of the Peace*. The Keynesian Revolution, to use the title of an early postwar book by Lawrence Klein, swept aside the neoclassical paradigm of Alfred Marshall, which had assumed that the normal state of a capitalist economy without signficant interference by the state was one of full employment. Any recessions or slumps, according to the neoclassical paradigm, were formerly considered as "deviations" from the normal state of affairs— one of "full employment equilibrium."

In revising his own ideas, Lord Keynes no doubt benefited enormously from the thinking of his young economist colleague Joan Robinson, who helped put him back on the track whenever he reverted to pre–*General Theory* thinking. Robinson had just completed her pre-Keynesian classic on the economics of imperfect competition or what we now would label "monopolistic competition." She would later disown this classic along with the actual practice of Keynesian economics in postwar Britain and the United States, eventually coining the term that is the title of this book to describe the U.S. economic policymaking after World War II.[1] Robinson also recognized the fact that the basic ideas of the *General Theory* had first appeared three years earlier in the Polish-language writings of Michal Kalecki.[2] Both books were of course responding to the Great Depression and the failure of free-market forces to extricate the advanced capitalist world from its doldrums.

The British interpretation of Bastard Keynesianism is summarized nicely in the *New Palgrave*, the four-volume economics encyclopedia, which was organized and edited by Robinson's young colleague, John Lord Eatwell.[3] Bastard Keynesianism regards as illegitimate (and hence bastardly) the interpretation of Keynes's *General Theory* simply as an "economics of disequilibrium." According to Geoffrey Harcourt, the contributor on this subject, "an equilibrium position has been shown to exist within the bounds of traditional theory (i.e., the Samuelsonian neo-classical synthesis), so that Keynes has a place not so much as a theorist but as a sensible propagator and rationalizer of policies in the short period, over the cycle, and *perhaps* permanently, as the average level of unemployment reflected a permananent tendency to a deficiency in aggregate demand" [emphasis added].

Keynesian principles were to be used countercyclically to reduce the volatility of the so-called business cycle but the long-run implications of the *General Theory*—such as the need for investment planning or the euthanasia of the rentier—were to be conveniently forgotten or minimized as to their implications. Just as Keynesian economics, as interpreted by Alvin Hansen in the United States, became the basis for the secular stagnation hypothesis in the late thirties, Bastard Keynesianism in the United States and Canada took on distinctly North American flavors, as we shall see in our concluding chapters.[4] Table 1 contrasts the key opposite positions of Classical Keynesianism and Bastard Keynesianism.

It has been said that anyone who received an economics education before Keynes's *General Theory* could never really understand Keynesian economics. It is also true that the initial book reviews of the *General Theory* by most of the top economists of that day (even including that of Alvin Hansen, his eventual U.S. disciple) were lukewarm or critical.

As Keynes recognized in the *General Theory* (p. 293), there was a division between the theory of the individual firm or industry, on the one hand, and the theory of output and employment as a whole. Until the *General Theory*, most economists—following the demise of the early classical economists—concentrated on what later became known as "microeconomics" or the theory of the firm or industry, assuming that the whole was simply the sum of its parts. Although the term "macroeconomics" was apparently the brainchild of Lawrence Klein in 1946, emphasis shifted in the years after 1936 to the determination of output and employment as a whole, or more popularly to gross national product (GNP).[5]

By 1940, Simon Kuznets was developing the rules of the game for the computation of national income and product accounts, a new measure of what was happening to the U.S. economy as a whole.

Table 1
Comparison of Classical Keynesian with Bastard Keynesian Model

Classical Keynesian Position	*Bastard Keynesian Position*
1. Advocates movement toward "euthanasia of the rentier"	1. Accepts the administration of the "highest real interest rates since the birth of Christ" (Helmut Schmidt)
2. Treats bankers as a "special interest group," one that should be neutralized	2. Endorses a stringent monetary policy, where interest rates are frequently raised to "cool off an overheated economy," which is assumed to be the normal state of affairs
3. Regards unemployment of labor and capital as the principal economic problem. Worries about deflationary tendencies	3. Considers inflation to be the principal problem, one that is reinforced by statistics that exaggerate the inflation problem and minimize the unemployment problem
4. Regards saving as a passive variable and accepts the "paradox of thrift." Savings discouraged as long as genuine full employment is not realized. As income rises, disguised savings will "crowd in" and become available for investment	4. Considers a higher rate of saving as necessary or a precondition for more investment. Government deficits are assumed to "crowd out" savings and investment
5. No bias in favor of military spending	5. If government spending increases, it must be military or labeled as such. An offensive posture could require troops stationed abroad as "permanent tourists," which contributes to balance-of-payments problems
6. Nonmercantilist approach to foreign trade and aid. The fruits of trade are imports and the costs are exports	6. Use of foreign trade and aid as employment creators. Beggar-thy-neighbor policies are practiced, especially by Japan and Germany

7. No bias toward devaluations or depreciations of currency to price country back into world markets. Welcoming of revaluations and strengthened currency

7. Bias toward devaluations or depreciations of currency to create employment. Avoidance of revaluations

8. Emphasizes long-range developments such as approach to stationary state and environmentally friendly policies

8. Emphasizes short- and medium-run problems and use of monetary and fiscal policy to minimize sharp fluctuations or "business cycles"

9. Progressive taxation to encourage consumption

9. Proportional or regressive taxation to encourage savings

10. Goal is to create exemplary society that others may wish to emulate

10. Imposing twentieth-century policies and institutions (balanced budgets, progressive taxation, anti-inflation austerity and reduced role of government) on remainder of the world, and using IMF to administer this policy

11. Supply-side economics is nineteenth-century thinking, when it worked reasonably well. If applied in the latter half of the twentieth century, it is like asking a ninety-year-old man to go jogging

11. Supply-side economics will release untapped resources that are fettered by too much government

Although Kuznets was important in collecting statistics and drawing up the accounting rules for the determination of gross national product—for which he was awarded a Nobel Prize—he never really appreciated the Keynesian message. Thus, his study of income distribution in the late 1940s concluded that there was a supposed tendency of movement toward greater income equality in the long run, as Alfred Marshall had predicted at the turn of the century. His results no doubt reflected the effect of wartime full employment in the first half of the decade. Kuznets furthermore deplored these changes since they produced a tendency for savings to be inadequate. By no coincidence, this research for the NBER was sponsored by the insurance industry.

In my own education, I became part of the first generation of economists to receive a Keynesian education from the very beginning at the University of California at Berkeley. Among my first mentors in 1940 was Robert Aaron Gordon, who had just completed his Keynesian graduate education at Harvard. Upon my return to Berkeley after a four-year hiatus in the Pacific theater, the results of Roosevelt's pragmatic Keynesianism during World War II were in evidence everywhere. In the 1945 Pabst Blue Ribbon contest for the best postwar solution to our expected peacetime economic problems, the top essay winners (Herbert Stein and Leon Keyserling) were both Keynesians. About the only anti-Keynesian voice at the time was that of Arthur Burns, who correctly anticipated the postwar boom. But even Burns failed to predict the immediate postwar stagnation that was only brought to an end by the outbreak of the Korean War.[6] Milton Friedman became disenchanted with Keynesian economics while working in the Treasury Department in 1943 but was comparatively unknown at the time.

The great genius of Keynes was his ability to modify his ideas in response to changing circumstances. Both of his principal early books, *The Economic Consequences of the Peace* and *The Treatise on Money*, were contradicted by the thinking of the *General Theory*. *The Treatise on Money* is one of Milton Friedman's favorite books and allowed him to claim that "we are all Keynesians now" in the late 1960s. Although Keynes was certainly not the only economist to begin thinking in a different way—Oswald Mosley, Michal Kalecki, Korekijo Takahashi, and Lauchlin Currie were operating on a similar wavelength—his reputation as an Establishment Liberal thinker and practitioner was crucial to the eventual acceptance of his ideas. Almost fifty years after Keynes's death in 1946, George Soros—the Wall Street currency speculator and benefactor for capitalist causes in Eastern Europe—recognized that it's as if Keynes had never existed.[7] At a meeting of the Eastern Economic Association in 1993, Paul Davidson predicted that in forty years no one would have heard of one of his and my favorite economists, Joan Robinson.

Societies have been formed to commemorate and honor the works of both Michael and Karl Polanyi in Budapest and Montreal, respectively. There is the Joseph Schumpeter Society and the longer-running Henry George Society, but nothing similar for Keynes. To be sure, there are a number of fine biographies by Skidelsky, Moggridge, and Hession and the complete works of Keynes in thirty volumes, edited by Moggridge. But what strikes this writer as interesting is the great similarity of today's conventional economic wisdom with the ideas prevailing before the *General Theory*.[8]

Although none but a few crackpots or supply-siders seriously talk about a return to the gold standard or specie-backed money, the deflationary thinking behind the gold standard prevails. Serious people talk about achieving "zero inflation" even if it takes double-digit unemployment to bring this about. One country, New Zealand, has even included "zero inflation" in its constitution. The fact that it may take a little suffering in the short run to achieve growth in the long run is an idea that finds credence in both the former Soviet Union (shock therapy) and on the world stage generally, where it may be labeled sadomonetarism.[9]

Keynes made an important contribution to Catastrophe Theory, but not along the lines of many of today's practitioners writing in the journal of the CATO Institute. These current writers typically contend that government help simply worsens things.

According to Keynes (*General Theory*, p. 129), "pyramid building, earthquakes, even wars may serve to increase wealth, if the education of our statesmen on the principle of classical economics stands in the way of anything better." In recent years, the Florida hurricane (1991), the bombing of the World Trade Center in New York (1992), the Midwest floods (1993), the Los Angeles earthquake (1994), and the California floods (1995) have served in the long run as important stimulants to a chronically sluggish economy, leading one to surmise that as a result of these Acts of God, at least He must still be a Keynesian![10]

Two-thirds of U.S. senators seem to be pushing for a "balanced budget amendment," thereby largely removing fiscal policy completely from the economic policymakers' tool kit. In times of recession, governments pare their staffs or welcome developments that reduce wages, when economic history (such as the wage reductions of the German Brüning government in the early thirties) tells us that such movements are counterproductive. Central banks now make preemptive strikes against inflation when the principal long-run problem is deflation and deflationary expectations. To be sure, Soros seems to be right.

In the following chapters, we examine changes in U.S. economic thinking and policymaking since World War II. Although there are certain continuities between the economic policies of the various administrations, there are also differences. Generally speaking, the Republican administrations have put a higher priority on fighting inflation than on dealing seriously with the unemployment problem. Since it is assumed that excessive growth leads to inflation, this has produced somewhat higher growth in Democratic years, at least until the Reagan "7 Fat Years," when policies similar to those of the Kennedy-Johnson era were adopted. Unemployment has tended to be higher during Republican administrations while inflation seems somewhat higher in Democratic years, particularly during the Carter presidency.

Since inflation was also higher in the late Nixon period, it seems likely that the two main reactions of the OPEC cartel were the primary source of inflation in the '70s. The lower inflation rates of the '80s and '90s, on the other hand, reflect the relative weakness of oil prices in the face of growing world oil surpluses.[11] In addition, the growing secular shortage of jobs—in the interest of controlling inflation—had produced weaker increases in money wages and declining real wages since the early '70s.

Federal deficits have tended to be higher under Republican administrations, leading one to conclude that these are passive deficits coming primarily from the revenue side of the budget. The former assumption of a positive correlation between active federal deficits and demand-pull inflation no longer holds. In fact, it is precisely during the Reagan years that the passive deficit grew rapidly at the same time that inflationary expectations subsided.

In the course of the following chapters, the following points of conventional wisdom will be questioned.

(1) It is frequently assumed that Hitler came to power as a result of the German hyperinflation or that he solved the German unemployment problem by simply turning on military spending. In fact, the German hyperinflation was largely confined to the year 1923, the Weimar economy prospering without serious inflation for the remainder of the '20s until the downturn in the spring of 1929. The conventional prescription of the Brüning government in the early '30s was a reduction of wages by an average of 10 percent. This policy produced a much higher rate of unemployment in Germany than in the United States. Upon coming to power, Hitler rejected the other conventional tool of the time by refraining from devaluing the mark, which, in effect, would have lowered domestic wages relative to wages abroad. Instead, he embarked on a public works program of autobahns, which were to be filled ultimately by *Volkswagens*, or "people's cars." Keynesian deficit financing was practiced and interest rates (like wages) were held in check. Military spending occurred primarily after full employment was achieved in 1936. Keynes's introduction to the German edition of the *General Theory* correctly assumed that the German theoreticians would be "thirsty" for Keynesian economics, which explained the secret of their economic success.

(2) It is sometimes assumed that the postwar years in the United States were successful due to pent-up demand after World War II. While a recession was postponed until 1949, partly as a result of the Marshall Plan, the postwar years were sluggish and the U.S. economy didn't

grow significantly until the Korean War years. U.S. fiscal policy was especially tight as the monetary policy was unusually easy or weak in the early postwar years. U.S. economic growth, in contrast to that of Western Europe, was also relatively sluggish during the Eisenhower years, with three recessions, the last of which in 1960 probably prevented the earlier election of Richard Nixon. Canadian growth was the most sluggish of all the G-7 countries, their economy failing to grow rapidly until after the devaluation of the Canadian dollar in 1962. Both U.S. and Canadian economists today frequently describe their economies in the 1950s as "prosperous," thereby reflecting mass amnesia.

(3) It is assumed that the Vietnam War produced the typical full employment results associated with wartime. In fact, there was considerable slack during most of the war, low profits (hence no need for an excess profits tax), and sluggish growth after 1968. If the U.S. economy was overheated during World War II, it was underheated during the Vietnam War. The Korean war was "just right."

(4) It is assumed that when the United States closed the gold window and opted for fluctuating exchange rates on August 15, 1971, it was brought about by weakness in the U.S. economy. In fact, it was a political decision designed by the Paul Volcker group working under secretary of the treasury John Connally. The objective was to ensure the reelection of Richard Nixon and reflected the relative strength of the U.S. economy to impose a revaluation of currency on its stronger trading partners, particularly Japan and West Germany. The subsequent decisions by OPEC to restore and improve their terms of trade in 1973 and 1979 produced great instability and weakness in the overall growth of world trade during the next decades. The elimination of fixed rates of exchange produced less concern over the balance-of-payments problem in the United States (as Milton Friedman had predicted), but the costs are still being felt, particularly in the recent breakdown of the European Monetary System, an attempt by Western Europe to "go it alone" after 1979 with respect to fixed exchange rates.[12] The Mexican peso crisis of 1995 was also a reflection of the instability of the floating exchange-rate system.

(5) There is continued belief in the so-called business cycle, the regularities in the ups and downs in economic activity studied for many years by the National Bureau of Economic Research under the leadership of Wesley Clair Mitchell. It is assumed that a certain predictability of economic activity can be obtained by studying the historic regularities or periodicity of fluctuations in economic activity. Recessions are supposedly automatically followed by expansions in economic activity, which bring about increased inflationary pressures, requiring attempts by government (or the Fed) to cool off an overheated economy. In my

view, about the only predictable development today is the "political business cycle" as forecast by Michal Kalecki during World War II. Increasingly, modern political democracies have attempted to stimulate the economy before elections and thereby assure the reelection of the incumbent party.

Instead of assuming the periodicity of fluctuations, we should, in my view, pay more attention to the secular or long-term developments or trends. By following a chronic policy of deflating the economy, we have for some time merely substituted supply-side inflation for the classical demand-pull inflation. At long last, we are approaching price stability at the cost of double-digit unemployment throughout most of the advanced industrial world. Although the advanced capitalist system has produced great microeconomic efficiency, it has also produced significant macroeconomic inefficiency. The inability of the United States to reduce seriously the military-industrial complex, despite the ending of the Cold War and the Russians' ability to reduce their military expenditures by approximately 70 percent, is the most obvious manifestation of this problem.

Zealots who believe in "zero inflation" now call for a preemptive strike against a phantom inflation. This dangerous game will eventually produce deflation followed by deflationary expectations. At this juncture, we should all head for the hills!

BASTARD KEYNESIANISM

Classical Keynesian Thinking

What were the basic characteristics or assumptions of Keynes's new way of thinking? Most important was the recognition of the failure of Say's Law. Earlier in the nineteenth century J.B. Say had convinced most economists that Thomas Malthus's fear of a "general glut" was unfounded. Subsequent economists during the following century assumed that "supply created its own demand." But the Great Depression represented a general glut throughout the advanced capitalist world, one that resulted in unprecedented unemployment of both labor and capital, and mass destruction of perfectly useful gifts of nature in a futile attempt to minimize the glut.

Some wag has defined an economist as someone who has seen something work in practice and then proceeds to make it work in theory. In some respects, this may have applied to Keynes, who was certainly aware of the tremendous economic miracle of Adolf Hitler in reducing unemployment from over 30 percent when he took office in 1933 to 1 percent by 1936, the year in which the German edition of the *General Theory* appeared.[1] In his special introduction to the German edition, Keynes recognized how "thirsty" the Germans must be for his "general theory," which would also apply to "national socialism."[2]

One of the features of Hitler's economy that also shows up in the *General Theory* is the neutralization of monetary policy. Like other populists, Hitler had a special aversion to interest as a form of income since he considered this return to capital to be "parasitic." Keynes in the *General Theory* has only a few references to monetary policy, and in one instance, he prescribed a lowering of interest rates in what we would later refer to as an overheated economy.[3] He also prescribed the "eutha-nasia of the rentier" or the eventual elimination of real interest in a mature capitalist economy. Subsequently, Keynes's disciple and early biographer, Sir Roy Harrod, would also suggest the abandonment of interest as a category of income to pacify postwar socialists in Great Britain.[4]

Like Hitler, Keynes in the mid-1930s preferred nationalist rather than internationalist solutions to economic problems. Hitler overruled Hjalmar Schacht and his other German advisers who advocated a devaluation of the German mark, something that became very popular internationally after Great Britain's successful devaluation of the pound in 1931.[5] Germany was to be as autarkic or nonmercantilist as possible and actually ran huge import surpluses or trade deficits with Eastern Europe once the Germans had regained full employment and had become a "suction economy," a useful term of Janos Kornai to describe a seller's market economy.[6]

There is a great irony in the fact that Keynes was the principal architect of the postwar international economic system as a result of his leadership at Bretton Woods in 1944. The offspring of this conference were the International Monetary Fund and the World Bank, both lead-ing centers of pre-Keynesian or monetarist thinking in the postwar years. In the words of Frances Stewart, "Even though the intentions of the Bretton Woods fathers were Keynesian, the institutions they created have turned out to be anti-Keynesian."[7]

The so-called paradox of thrift was also an important ingredient of classical Keynesian thinking. Under conditions of less than full employ-ment, the attempt to save more and consume less might actually pro-duce less aggregate saving. Although Keynes didn't ignore saving, he did think of it as a passive variable compared to the relatively active investment.[8] Consumption could be safely encouraged through higher "propensities to consume," which U.S. economists such as Alvin Han-sen translated into the need for a more equal distributon of income under U.S. conditions, assumed to be subject to "secular stagnation."[9]

Keynes's small book *How to Pay for the War* (1940) reversed gears and advocated an increase in the rate of saving as the wartime British economy would soon get back to full employment. According to Keynes, this forced savings in the form of savings bonds (paying 2½ percent interest) would eventually be useful in facilitating the transition to a peacetime economy. This book, according to Robert Skidelsky, is surprisingly libertarian and was approved by von Hayek.[10]

Like Hitler, Keynes saw nothing wrong with deficit financing, partic-ularly if there was significant unemployment. If the economy got back to full employment as a result of greater government expenditures for investment (infrastructure) or consumption and tax reductions, presumably there might be surpluses developing in the government budgets so that there might be a rough balancing of the budget over the so-called business cycle. Although Hitler was relatively benign in his treatment of profits, it was expected in his Four-year Plans (beginning in 1936) that the private capitalist would not go on strike, or withhold investment. In some cases, public investment in automobile production (Volkswagen) or steel (Hermann Goering Steel Works in Linz) received a high priority.[11]

Franklin Delano Roosevelt and the New Deal before World War II showed relatively little influence from the *General Theory*. Although interest rates were generally very low by the mid-1930s, Roosevelt went along with Congress in eliminating the influence of the Treasury—and accepting the increased role of the representatives of the Federal Reserve Banks—on the Federal Reserve Board in 1935. By 1937, fiscal policy became very tight—partly due to the introduction of the social security tax—as Roosevelt assumed that government spending could be pared and the budget balanced, as it was in 1937.

During the preceding year, the Federal Reserve, under the leadership of Marriner Eccles, had doubled reserve requirements, supposedly to fight inflation. The result was calamitous. The 1938 recession occurred well before unemployment dropped to single-digit figures and was one of the sharpest declines in economic activity on record. The unemployment rate shot up again from 14 percent to 19 percent. Eventually, aid to Britain—Lend-Lease and "Bundles for Britain"—produced some upturn, but the United States still suffered from double-digit unemployment on the eve of Pearl Harbor. It seems clear that Rooseveltian "pump priming," or an attempt to jump-start the economy in the 1930s, bore little resemblance to Classical Keynesian theory.

Economic Thinking during and after World War II

Following the Japanese attack and Germany's declaration of war on the United States, the nation rallied around FDR to produce the arsenal for democracy. Output rose more rapidly than during any other time on record. Aggregate consumption increased during this period from $67.4 billion in 1939 to $122 billion in 1945.[1] Rates of unemployment also fell to record lows with a 1.2 percent unemployment rate in 1944, the last full year of the war.[2] Prices in this "guns-and-butter" economy were controlled effectively by the Office of Price Administration, headed for a time by John Kenneth Galbraith. Wages weren't frozen until six months later than prices, resulting in a profit squeeze reinforced by an excess profits tax. Under these circumstances there was a more egalitarian distribution of income by the end of the war than was the case in the 1930s. It was this temporary wartime change that resulted in Simon Kuznets's premature conclusion in 1949 that the capitalist income distribution was becoming more equal over time.

The agricultural surpluses—built up before the war by New Deal programs to raise the support prices that farmers received—were rapidly depleted in this full employment economy, and per capita food consumption reached a peak in 1945 that still stands today, all without food stamps. Recorded inflation was minimal, although it was recognized that considerable forced saving was taking place and there was significant pent-up demand by the end of the war. Any war bonds that were not sold to the public by the Treasury were automatically bought up by the Federal Reserve in a so-called monetization of the debt.

Beginning in early 1942, the Fed was rendered inactive or neutral with respect to monetary policy and nominal interest rates were thereafter "pegged," or capped, at roughly 2 percent. To achieve this unprecedented easy monetary policy, the Fed was compelled to buy excess bonds continually to support the price of bonds and keep interest rates at or below the pegged level. By the end of the war—as a result of this "soft-budget constraint"—the national debt was also at a new record, equivalent to 130 percent of the gross national product of that time. The problem of servicing this huge debt probably accounts for the extension of the pegged interest rates until the Treasury Accord of March 1951. Ironically, the pre-Hitler power of West German bankers was restored in a program to de-Nazify the German economy by John McCloy, the High Commissioner for Occupied Germany (HICOG) by 1948.[3] In a further attempt to rid the Germans of Keynesian or Hitlerian influence, the tool of Keynesian deficit-financing was withheld by the postwar constitution until after the first major German recession in 1966–67.

During the war, there was a great deal of thinking about what would happen after the war. Since World War II had pulled the capitalist world (except for Germany, Italy, and Japan) out of the Great Depression, it was natural to assume that, with the ending of the war, the economy would slip back into some sort of depression. At one point in the latter part of the war, Vice President Henry Wallace reported in his diary that a guest at one of his dinner parties (possibly Harry Magdoff) had suggested a declaration of war against the Atlantic Ocean.

There were two principal schools of thought about how to treat the Russians after the war. One school was located primarily in the office of the secretary of the treasury, Henry Morgenthau, and included Harry Dexter White, who collaborated tempestuously with Keynes at Bretton Woods. They proposed both a "pastoralization," or deindustrialization, of Germany and a huge loan to Stalin to help the USSR recover from the serious damage inflicted by the Fascist invaders. The other school, located in the State Department, was friendlier to Germany and suspicious of the Russians. The thinking of George Kennan is the best representative of this school and would eventually result in his famous "Mr. X" article in *Foreign Affairs* (1947) urging the containment of the Soviet Union. At the end of the war, a Soviet request for a $1 billion postwar loan was mysteriously "lost" by the State Department.[4]

The problem of possible postwar reparations was dealt with by Jacob Viner, a consultant with the Treasury, in a seminal article in *Foreign Affairs* in July 1943. Viner warned policymakers not to repeat the mistake of the Versailles Treaty, which attempted to levy $30 billion in reparations on the Weimar Republic. Viner recognized that in a real sense these reparations had never been paid and that the Dawes Plan loan only enabled the Germans to go through the motions of paying reparations until the "Moratorium" of 1931.[5] In the words of Peter Temin, "Germany managed to avoid paying reparations by a variety of economic and political maneuvers that succeeded in postponing its obligations until they could be repudiated entirely."[6]

The problem of obtaining reparations was hardly that claimed by Keynes in his *Economic Consequences of the Peace* (1919). Keynes thought that the reparations bill had been too draconian whereas the later Keynesians—Bertil Ohlin, Etienne Mantoux, and John Foster Dulles in 1921—recognized that the real problem was the inability of the U.S. economy to absorb the reparations or repayment of war debts.[7] Keynes refused to commit himself on this problem after World War II. However, in view of his earlier critique of the Versailles Treaty, he would have undoubtedly approved of the later Marshall Plan, which involved one of the victors, the United States, paying reparations of $5 billion to the loser, (West) Germany.

As mentioned previously, Keynes was instrumental in the formation of the international monetary institutions of the postwar world. It was hoped that the autarky of the Great Depression was only an anomaly and the postwar situation would involve a flourishing of world trade. It was decided, both by Keynes and White, that "fixed" exchange rates would reduce the risk of international business, and the IMF was organized to supervise these fixed rates and determine when a devaluation (or revaluation) of any fixed rate was appropriate.[8] Less developed countries were supposed to seek permission to devalue in order to price themselves back into world markets. More developed countries, like Great Britain or France—both of which had sophisticated money markets and currency speculators—would devalue first and then notify the IMF. If a devaluation were approved, the country was expected to pursue austerity or deflationary programs, since, according to legend, devaluations were supposedly inflationary because of immediately higher import prices.[9]

U.S. business organizations such as the National Association of Manufacturers and the United States Chamber of Commerce, which had been strongholds of protectionist thinking in the 1930s, began to push the idea that freer trade was good for the United States now that we were the dominant and most productive economy in the world. As with Great Britain in the nineteenth century, the most advanced country can always take the lead when it comes to freer trade. Eventually, Bastard Keynesians would become neomercantilist, no doubt encouraged by the *General Theory*'s benign treatment of mercantilism. As a result, they worried about the U.S. trade deficits or import surpluses, conveniently forgetting the "mature creditor" hypothesis popularized by Paul Samuelson.[10]

Eugene Varga, writing in Moscow in 1945, and Michal Kalecki, writing now from Great Britain in 1944, both concluded that the U.S. capitalists had learned how to make Keynesian economics work as a result of the World War II experience. Varga was subsequently ostracized by Stalin (who pinned his hopes on the collapse of capitalism after the war) and lived under a cloud until after Stalin's death in 1953. Kalecki's recognition of the "political business cycle" assumed, among other things, that the postwar capitalists would not opt for a full employment noncyclical model, despite its success during the war, since a certain amount of unemployment of labor helps in disciplining wage demands. In other words, the single capitalist would lean toward a higher rate of profit for himself or herself rather than a greater aggregate amount of profits for all capitalists.

Still another important article written by Abba Lerner appeared in 1943. Lerner's "functional finance" represented a logical extension of Keynesian economics, although it was not originally recognized as such by Lord Keynes. As David Colander pointed out in 1984, it required a personal confrontation between Keynes and Lerner, who considered himself a Keynesian and was shocked by his mentor's failure to recognize his offspring. Functional finance asserts that federal taxation is unnecessary for revenue purposes since the monetization of the debt—printing and selling Treasury bonds to the Fed—is a suitable alternative. Orthodox economists would describe this as "turning on the printing presses." The only logical reason for taxation is to keep down consumption, as was the case in the full employment economy of World War II. Here again we have an economist looking at what we were doing successfully and then seeking a theory for the practice.

THE TRANSITION FROM WARTIME PLANNING TO A PEACEFUL MARKET

Despite the fears of economic decline after the war, the immediate transition to a peacetime economy was smoother than it had been after World War I. After the earlier war, there was a sharp drop in economic activity in the 1920–21 recession. After World War II, the GI Bill absorbed 1.5 million former servicemen and women, who decided to invest in their education. For those unable to find a job or go back to school there was "52-20," 20 dollars a week for a year in payments that were not unlike unemployment compensation. Women, who had flooded into the labor market during the war assisted by temporary government child care programs, were eased out of their jobs and encouraged to reproduce in the postwar baby boom and the rapid suburbanization of the U.S. economy.

The pent-up demand accumulated during the war as a result of effective price controls, and financing through the sales of bonds rather than taxes, absorbed a great deal of potential unemployment. Since no private automobiles had been produced during the four years of war, there were long waiting lists for cars. At the same time, the automobile manufacturers priced their output below equilibrium, thereby forego-ing short-term potential profits. Under the circumstances, it was possi-ble for a buyer to take delivery on a car and drive it around the block before selling it for $1,000 more than was paid for it.[11]

In 1946, a Republican-controlled House of Representatives decided to administer "shock therapy" on the postwar economy by scuttling wage and price controls. For the next three years, there was an approx-imately 10 percent annual increase in the general price level as some of the pent-up demand released demand-pull inflation that had been bottled up by the price controls. Since the nominal interest rate was still pegged at 2 percent, the real interest rate for the period 1946 to 1948 averaged minus 8 percent.

The creation of the Employment Act of 1946 and birth of the Council of Economic Advisers (CEA) reflected Congress's fear of falling back into the Great Depression. Its first chairman was Edwin Nourse, but one of its members was Leon Keyserling, who had been instrumental in drafting the legislation. In fact, part of the wording in the legislation was taken from his second-prize Pabst essay. Nourse and Keyserling differed greatly on the purpose of the CEA and on the relative priorities of the inflation and full employment problems. Keyserling favored a "political" CEA, whereas Nourse thought that there was a possibility of economists remaining neutral on economic policy. Like Paul Samuel-son, he denied that there were separate Republican and Democratic eco-nomics. Nourse was more worried about inflation; Keyserling was more committed to full employment. Nourse was more inclined to bring the Fed back into the picture by allowing for a tightening of monetary policy.

There was little recognition among economists of the trade-off be-tween inflation and unemployment, and virtually no one predicted what turned out to be the subsequent secular or long-term postwar inflation. The price level in 1940 was about the same as it had been at the beginning of the nineteenth century. Over the long haul, prices tended to rise during our wars, but decline thereafter. After World War I, for example, prices gently declined in the 1920s (after the immediate postwar deflation) before the severe deflation of the 1930s. On the eve of World War II, the price level was still well below that of 1929. By early 1949, Nourse had convinced President Truman of the necessity for a tax increase, but Keyserling urged caution. The 1949 recession proved Nourse wrong, and Keyserling replaced him, first as acting chairman.[12] The unemployment rate rose to over 7 percent and the consumer price index actually fell in 1949, the only year, other than 1955, when this has occurred since World War II.

In addition to the Marshall Plan, which eventually underwrote the shipment of more than $13 billion worth of goods to Western Europe spread over four years, Truman introduced foreign aid in the form of Point 4 of his proposal for saving Greece and Turkey for the "Free World." Greece had been allocated to Great Britain when Churchill and Stalin divided up Eastern Europe into spheres of influence in 1944. Apparently the Greek Communists were unimpressed by this deal when they began their civil war. Stalin made good on his promise to Churchill by refusing to assist the Greek Communists, and Greece remained in the Western camp, in part because of the U.S. aid contained in Point 4.

Thereafter foreign aid became a permanent characteristic of U.S. foreign policy and was copied to some extent by most of the other advanced capitalist countries.[13] Such assistance by the United States was politically inspired and could be withdrawn as punishment for any underdeveloped country that failed to vote with the U.S. majority in the United Nations. It became part of the employment-creating Bastard Keynesianism that developed throughout the advanced capitalist system during the postwar years. U.S. grain surpluses, which had been rotting in Liberty Ships sitting in the Hudson River, were eventually moved to Third World countries under Public Law 480. Payments were ostensibly made by the recipients in nonconvertible local currencies, which had only limited use by businessmen and scholars operating in these countries. At one point, Ambassador Pat Moynihan later ordered the burning of $2 billion worth of these superfluous nonconvertible rupees when he was in India.[14]

Although the postwar economy of the United States was stabilized by the pent-up demand and forced savings built up during the war, the Marshall Plan and Point 4 and its successor, Foreign Aid (later the Agency for International Development), the transition to a peacetime economy was remarkably sluggish. Real income in 1950 was little higher than it had been in 1945, and it wasn't until the Korean War boom that the economy overtook the annual production at the end of World War II.

This sluggishness and growing underutilization of resources was especially worrisome to acting chairman Leon Keyserling, who was responsible for the economics underlying NSC-68, a secret National Security Council memorandum drawn up by Keyserling and Paul Nitze in early 1950.[15] According to Keyserling, there was no reason why the United States couldn't increase military spending by threefold and still have increases in consumption. Keyserling, a "guns-and-butter" economist, never admitted to being a Keynesian, but preferred calling himself a "pragmatist."[16] Using U.S. World War II experience as a guide, he realized that there was a tremendous underutilized potential in the U.S. economy that allowed us (but not the Russians) to have our cake and eat it too. In subsequent years, Keyserling never saw an increase in military spending that he didn't support.

THE ECONOMICS OF THE KOREAN WAR

Although there was little chance that there was enough political support in Congress for NSC-68, the outbreak and prosecution of the Korean War served to accomplish the same purpose. During the war, military spending increased by well over threefold, the unemployment rate dropped to 2.7 percent by 1953, and consumption went up at the same time. The Korean War was financed with very little increase in the national debt. In fact, during the first year of the war, there was a surplus in the budget in contrast to the deficit produced by the Truman recession in 1949. This was a good example of an expansion of the economy absorbing a passive deficit by increasing tax revenues.

There was some speculative inflation in raw materials prices during the first few months of the war, which resulted in formal price controls, administered primarily by lawyers rather than economists, as during World War II. Personal income taxes were increased slightly and an excess profits tax was reintroduced.

Bankers had begun a campaign to restore the prewar independence of the Federal Reserve System and to break with the pegged nominal interest rate that had prevailed since 1942. The Chairman of the Fed, Marriner Eccles, who had enthusiastically supported the demonetization of the U.S. economy during the war, was gradually eased out of his position of power, first being demoted to deputy chairman under Thomas McCabe.

The potential inflation associated with the Korean War helped justify the Treasury Accord of March 1951, which ended the pegged interest rate and ushered in the return of an independent monetary policy. Leading U.S. economists, including Paul Samuelson, argued that U.S. policymakers could use a tighter monetary policy as a tool in fighting inflation. The chairman of the CEA, Leon Keyserling, opposed the Treasury Accord, but many leading economists, meeting at Princeton, gave their seal of approval. After Keyserling was removed as chairman by the Eisenhower administration, he spent the rest of his intellectual life arguing for lower interest rates. One of his many critical pamphlets dealt with the *Toll of Rising Interest Rates*.[17]

Eisenhower and the Rejection of Military Keynesianism

Keyserling's Military Keynesianism received a setback with the election of President Dwight Eisenhower in 1952. Eisenhower soon made good on two of his campaign promises: (1) he ended the war in Korea by making concessions to the Chinese that Truman said he could have made six months earlier; and (2) he disbanded the price controls that had been put into effect after prices of raw materials rose owing to the speculation in the early months of the war. Surprisingly, when the price controls were eliminated, there was no evidence of pent-up demand as there was after World War II, and prices actually dropped a bit thereafter.

The new Republican administration was committed to market forces and briefly threatened to dissolve the Council of Economic Advisers, a move that President Reagan would also toy with after his reelection in 1984. The same threat came from Gingrich Republicans in 1995. Instead, Eisenhower finally appointed Arthur Burns, an expert on monetary policy, to head the CEA, thereby confirming Keyserling's thesis that the Council of Economic Advisers should reflect the political economy of the administration. Burns had earlier distinguished himself as a non-Keynesian in 1946 by rejecting the prevailing Keynesian economics consensus, arguing—correctly, as it turned out—that there was little danger of a postwar recession.

As a former general, Eisenhower was able to hold a lid on military spending of about $40 to 50 billion yearly, down from Korean War levels but more than three times higher than it was before NSC-68 and the Korean conflict. By the end of the Republican administration, the Kennedy presidential campaign would be emphasizing the phantom "missile gap" and the Pentagon would be supporting the Democrats. In his farewell address to the nation, Eisenhower sagely warned his fellow citizens against the so-called military-industrial complex, which he had controlled only with difficulty.

During this period, nonmilitary expenditures by the federal government were frequently justified by the Cold War. Eisenhower's ambitious highway building program was passed as the Federal Aid Highway Act in 1956, which produced the National System of Interstate and Defense highways, now bearing Ike's name. Later, after the Russians had startled the world with Sputnik in 1957, federal assistance to higher education increased under the guise of keeping up with the Russians. By the end of the decade, the relatively sluggish growth and three recessions in the United States—in contrast to the rapid growth of the Soviet economy—had given birth to the economics of "growthmanship," or examining the role that government spending and taxation should play in keeping the United States ahead of the Russians.

In 1959, Eisenhower single-handedly invited Premier Khrushchev to visit the United States, where he would be suitably impressed by the fruits of capitalism and the productivity of the Iowa cornfields. Khrushchev addressed the Economic Club in New York City and reassured his audience of businessmen that the U.S. economy had nothing to fear from a reduction in military spending. Up to this point, spokespersons for the USSR, including local Marxists, had argued that capitalism was stabilized, if not strengthened, by military spending. Thereafter all Soviet propagandists emphasized the deleterious effect of military spending on the U.S. economy. This consensus was mirrored in the United States in the thinking and writings of both the non-Communist Seymour Melman and the Communist Party spokesperson, Victor Perlo.

The first Eisenhower recession occurred after the Korean War in 1954 despite the fact that the Korean War income tax surcharge was quickly dropped. The second recession occurred in 1958 and produced the largest postwar deficit in the federal budget of fiscal 1959. It is the first striking example of recessions producing large passive deficits resulting from the decline in tax revenues. Under such conditions, unemployed labor and capital stop contributing their revenues to the federal budget and instead receive unemployment compensation. To get out of this recession, Eisenhower confined himself to a cameo appearance on TV in which he urged consumers to go out and buy automobiles. Unfortunately, this was the year of the Edsel. Later, as the Eisenhower administration was due to be replaced, a third recession developed with unemployment rising to 7 percent. Eisenhower refused to play the political business-cycle game of stimulating the economy to achieve the election of Richard Nixon, who lost by only a narrow margin. Later, we shall see that Nixon learned from this experience, as well as the Canadian events of 1962 (i.e., the effects of the devaluation of the overvalued Canadian dollar).

Despite the growing slack in the U.S. economy, there still seemed to be a continuation of some mild inflation, leading economists to look for some explanation other than the conventional demand-pull theory that covered wartime inflation. It was easy to see how too many dollars chasing too few goods could push up prices in a demand-pull inflation. But this situation hardly applied to the U.S. economy by 1960.

An important contributor to inflation theory had been Sumner Slichter in 1953. Slichter, a conservative professor at the Harvard Business School, had correctly predicted (like Arthur Burns) that there would be a postwar economic expansion. But he also argued that a certain amount of inflation—what we today should call a "natural rate of inflation"—might be tolerated to ease or facilitate advanced capitalist development. His dovish position on inflation shocked the business world, which could hardly imagine secular inflation. John Kenneth Galbraith, in his pathbreaking *The Affluent Society* (1957), assumed that it would be possible to control inflation with 7 percent unemployment. A New Zealand economist, A.W. Phillips, later published an article in *Economica*, in which he plotted the annual increases in money wages on the vertical axis and unemployment on the horizontal axis for the past century, obtaining a negative correlation or "trade-off" between these two variables. The implication of the Phillips curve (later drawn with the rate of inflation on the vertical axis) was that higher unemployment would help reduce inflationary pressure. Thus, there were now two types of inflation to worry about: old-fashioned demand-pull inflation and wage-push inflation coming from the supply side.

Meanwhile, an alternative paradigm was developing under the leadership of Milton Friedman and his Chicago School. They denied that there was any long-run trade-off between inflation and unemployment, as posited by the Phillips curve. Rather, workers would not be fooled by the "money illusion" and there was in the long run a vertical Phillips curve, at the so-called natural rate of unemployment (NAIRU), or no relationship in the long run. For Friedman, inflation is ultimately related to the supply of money, which reverted back to a belief in a modified quantity theory of money, which had previously been associated with Irving Fisher before World War I.[1] Friedman claimed to be able to predict the rate of inflation from a knowledge of the increase in the money supply with a suitable lag. The main problem would be one of finding the proper measure of the money supply and the length of the lag. To lick inflation it would first be necessary to convince the monetary authorities to "bite the bullet" or sharply restrict the growth of the money supply.

In the Cold War competition, the advanced capitalist system was becoming more conscious of the more egalitarian income distribution of the opposition. During the 1950s, any thought of conscious income redistribution was considered passé as a result of Kuznets's *Income Revolution* (1949), which had convinced the economics profession that capitalism was gradually producing a more equal income distribution. Galbraith apparently went along with this in recommending the use of a sales tax to raise revenue, despite its regressive reputation. Instead, he argued that more public spending—a characteristic of the non-capitalist system—could help equalize the income distribution. The work of Robert Lampman on changes in the distribution of income and wealth was the first to challenge the Kuznets position, which incidentally was also held much earlier by Alfred Marshall. But the greatest challenge came later from outside the economics fraternity, from a historian, Gabriel Kolko, who concluded that the income distribution was already becoming more unequal under capitalism, something that seems obvious in 1995.

The Cold War also began to affect our ideas on how to handle the problem of racial discrimination. The first example of affirmative action for blacks shows up in the thinking of Vice President Richard Nixon. In August 1953, after the Korean War, President Eisenhower issued Executive Order No. 10479, establishing a fifteen-member Committee on Government Contracts chaired by the vice president. This order reaffirmed the U.S. policy of promoting equal employment opportunity under government contracts, because all persons are "entitled to fair and equitable treatment in all aspects of employment on work paid for from public funds." The Committee on Government Contracts often attempted to foster minority employment by urging the hiring of blacks on a limited "preferential" basis (i.e., giving preference to a black applicant when a black and a white applicant were equally qualified). Generally speaking, the contracting agencies were unwilling to adopt the "firmer approach" of affirmative action recommended by committee chairman Nixon.

Eight years of Eisenhower laissez-faire, or nonmilitary, non-Keynesian policies, had produced an impasse. The lid on military spending led to sluggish economic growth and three recessions. At the same time, the economy of the USSR was apparently growing in an unprecedented fashion. The country was ready for growthmanship and the "New Economics" of the Kennedy-Johnson administrations.

The Return of Military Keynesianism under Kennedy-Johnson

John F. Kennedy's economic advisers initially assumed that when the president talked about what Americans could do for their country in his inaugural address, he was suggesting a tax increase. Sanity prevailed after it was realized that the economic advisers were facing an economy operating with 7 percent unemployment originating in Eisenhower's third recession.[1] The fastest way to jump-start the economy would be to make good on Kennedy's campaign promise to remove the Eisenhower lid on defense spending. After Kennedy's early confrontation with Khrushchev in Vienna, military spending increased. During JFK's first two years, military spending, space expenditures, and foreign aid all grew more rapidly than gross national product.[2]

Likewise, after the Vienna confrontation, Premier Khrushchev returned to Moscow and the USSR soon announced an unprecedented midyear (July 1, 1961) increase in defense expenditures of 44 percent. Within the next several years, there was a sharp drop in the Soviet growth rates along with a significant increase in the expansion of the U.S. economy. The underlying thinking behind Keyserling's NSC-68 was materializing. The "free lunch economy" of the United States could increase military spending and enjoy gains in both consumption and investment as well. The "no free lunch" economy of the USSR would suffer losses in both investment and consumption if it attempted to match U.S. military gains, as it did after 1961.[3]

It can be assumed that the Soviet Union had been able to restrict its military spending of the fifties in favor of more investment and consumption, thereby increasing its growth at a rapid pace. The secrecy surrounding what the Russians were doing in the 1950s was therefore an advantage that was lost in the '60s when the United States developed its satellites or "spies in the sky."[4] No longer could the Russians afford to neglect their military-industrial complex and use the released resources for consumption and investment.

The chairman of Kennedy's CEA was Walter Heller, who was given credit for developing the "New Economics." These policies showed the influence of Keynes, albeit in its Military and Commercial Keynesian form, to use a term coined by Robert Lekachman. One of Heller's first acts was to dispatch a group of economists to Paris to see why Western Europe was booming in contrast to the Eisenhower stagnation. The first achievement of the new CEA was to develop the concept of "fiscal drag." A calculation was made of the hypothetical balance in the federal budget if there were only a 4 percent (assumed at the time to be the "full employment" rate of unemployment), rather than the existing 7 percent, unemployment. This calculation produced a budget surplus of $9 billion, which indicated that tax rates were too high and were producing a fiscal drag.

It was fairly easy to convince Congress that business taxes should be reduced. There was a major change, the introduction of the investment tax credit, supplemented by the institutionalization of rapid depreciation write-offs in 1962. These subsidies for investment were used by Heller to justify his assertion in the 1980s that he was the first *practicing* supply-side economist, although he didn't have the imagination to think up the catchy label later adopted by economic advisers in the Reagan administration.

As mentioned earlier, there was a growing belief both in cost-push inflation and in the need for institutions that would limit money wage increases to the prevailing increases in labor productivity. The wage-price guideposts of early 1962—sometimes referred to as an "incomes policy"—provided for an annual 3.2 percent increase in money wages, which was more or less in line with the gains in labor productivity being achieved in the early 1960s. If organized labor would accept these guideposts, they could expect to realize zero inflation and therefore also real wage gains of the same magnitude as the increase in labor productivity. The steel companies were expected to cooperate in this policy. When United States Steel increased the prices of steel in the spring of 1962, President Kennedy was understandably incensed and forced a rollback in steel prices. Reporters called steel executives at 4:00 A.M. to learn their reaction to the president's position. Ironically, steel prices didn't hold even at the rollback level and declined in the fall of that year.

In June 1962, the president gave a graduation address at Yale University in which he denied the need to submit a balanced budget to Congress every year. He argued instead that there were times when an increase in the budget deficit would be needed to stimulate the economy. There were other times when it might be necessary to plan a surplus in the federal budget to cool off an overheated economy. Before this address, it had been customary for presidents to submit planned balanced budgets each year, even though the actual expenditures might eventually exceed the revenues by as much as $13 billion, as in fiscal 1959. These passive deficits were later to be contrasted with active or structural deficits at full employment.[5]

In addition to the cut in business taxes, Kennedy also planned to have an across-the-board 10 percent reduction in personal income taxes. A coalition of conservative Republicans and southern Democrats (headed by Wilbur Mills) succeeded in having his tax cut bottled up in committee until the assassination in November 1963. Early in the Johnson administration, the tax cut sailed through a contrite Congress and the economy took off. Economic journalists, such as Edwin L. Dale, wrote articles with such titles as "Are Recessions a Thing of the Past?"[6]

Euphoria prevailed, particularly as previously unemployed resources—both labor and capital—began to pay taxes and the federal deficit melted. At some point, there would presumably be a surplus at full employment and a fiscal "dividend" would arise. The problem of the administration would then become one of thinking up new programs to absorb the fiscal surplus. By 1965, jokesters in Washington were saying that the way to balance the budget was to reduce tax rates. It was this Democratic experience that supply-siders or Commercial Keynesians in the Reagan administration would later use to buttress their prediction that the budget would be balanced by 1984. At the same time, the Democrats seemed to be afflicted with mass amnesia with respect to this important experience.[7]

By the end of 1965, the United States was committing more resources to the Vietnam War while the economy approached the assumed full employment unemployment rate of 4 percent. The first tightening of monetary policy resulted from the December decision by the Fed, under the leadership of William McChesney Martin. This independent decision created considerable consternation in the Council of Economic Advisers—now headed by Gardner Ackley—which had been planning to use fiscal policy or an income tax increase to slow down what was presumed to be an overheating economy. President Johnson attempted to solve the problem by inviting representatives of the Fed and the CEA to discuss their differences at an economic summit meeting down on his ranch on the Pedernales River.

Fiscal policy was also tightened, but not by an income tax surcharge that the CEA was hoping to use. Instead, the withholding tax was made progressive (peaking at 18 percent) instead of the flat 14 percent that had previously been deducted from paychecks. Social Security taxes were increased as Medicare was introduced. In addition, the investment tax credit and rapid depreciation were abandoned in September 1966, which would presumably increase receipts from the corporation income tax. By the end of the year, the economy was obviously slowing down in the middle of a war, and the administration sheepishly reintroduced the investment tax credit only four months after its suspension. A monetary crunch cut into housing construction, and the higher interest rates were felt mainly by small businessmen in 1966.

By the first quarter of 1967, there was an actual reduction in real gross national product. A slight increase in real gross national product in the second quarter of the year prevented this year-long relative stagnation from being counted by the National Bureau of Economic Research as a full-scale recession, and it was labeled a "minirecession." But this was clearly a new phenomenon—a type of growth recession in the middle of a war when military spending was soaring. Pundits on Wall Street, such as Eliot Janeway, concluded that wars were no longer capable of stimulating the economy.[8] Partly as a result of the minirecession, Wall Street thereafter took a bullish view whenever there was a threat of peace breaking out in Vietnam.

This same year, the price-wage guidelines of 1962 began to unravel. On the surface, they seemed to have been highly successful. As it turned out, the increase in labor productivity had averaged 3.8 percent over five years rather than the projected 3.2 percent, and the price level was increasing by between 1 percent and 2 percent annually. Real wages were thus rising by only 2 percent rather than the 3.2 percent promised by the Kennedy guideposts or the 3.8 percent to which they were entitled. The declines in unit labor costs were resulting in a significant increase in profits relative to wages.

The problem with the guidelines was that the producers that had the capability of lowering prices, because they had above-average increases in labor productivity, such as automobile manufacturing, were subject to price "stickiness" on the downside. In some cases, increased advertising expenditures were an alternative to price reductions. The expected increase in the prices of services, which were incapable of increasing labor productivity by 3.2 percent, were not counterbalanced by the lowering of other prices.

Organized labor realized that it had been sold a bill of goods and thereafter began demanding money wage increases of at least 6 percent to make up for its previous failure to get its proportionate share of increased productivity. This occurred simultaneously with the sudden slowdown in increases in labor productivity, thereby producing rapid increases in unit labor costs. The *Economic Report of the President, 1968* conceded that "the rise in prices that did occur in that sluggish period [mid-1966 to mid-1967] was essentially a reflection of rising costs rather than excessive demand."

The Johnson administration and Congress were finally successful in imposing a 10 percent income tax surcharge on July 1, 1968, which produced a small short-term surplus in the budget for fiscal 1969, the last time this would occur. Mainstream economists assumed that this tax increase was two years too late. But it is difficult to see how any earlier tax increase would not have produced an ordinary recession, rather than the minirecession that occurred as a result of the tightening of both monetary and fiscal policy in 1966.

As it was, the Johnson surcharge no doubt contributed to the Nixon Recession in late 1969, despite the fact that one of Nixon's first acts was to phase out the Johnson surcharge. In addition, President Nixon got rid of the investment tax credit and (in stages) Johnson's attempt to control foreign investment, which was imposed in a futile attempt to reduce the balance-of-payments deficit, a problem that had occupied an important place in the fears of the Kennedy-Johnson advisers.

Early in the Kennedy years, the "dollar gap," which had been the characteristic of the 1950s as the countries of Western Europe recovered, gave way to its opposite—the "dollar glut." Western European countries were now fully capable of exporting to the United States, and our export surplus began to dwindle. The early responses of the Kennedy administration were protectionist, despite the fact that the administration was concomitantly pushing the Kennedy Round for freer trade in GATT. Foreign aid was "tied"—that is, recipients of foreign aid were forced to spend their foreign aid dollars in the United States. "Operation Twist" was designed to create a gap between short-term interest rates, which were intended to be high, thereby attracting foreigners' "hot money," and long-term interest rates, which would be low to stimulate domestic investment. U.S. tourists were limited in their purchases abroad by taxation of gifts exceeding a certain amount.

On the home front, our economic ideas on the role of women were changing. The Civil Rights Act of 1964 was the basis for the affirmative action programs for blacks that developed in response to rioting in the ghettos of the central cities. Although the women's liberation movement also developed beginning in the mid-1960s, women (and the handicapped) were not subject to affirmative action programs until after 1972. The female labor force participation rates began to rise as comparatively uneducated women came into the labor force and the gap between male and female average wages widened. The introduction of the "pill," along with the greater acceptance of women in labor unions and in nonunion jobs, triggered a sharp decline in fertility rates as the postwar baby boom ended.

Conversion of President Nixon to Nonmilitary Keynesianism

President Nixon, like his role model, Eisenhower, was committed to "free market" economics when he entered office. But he was also determined to extricate the United States from the Vietnam quagmire. The economy he inherited was assumed to be near full employment, as the official unemployment rate was below 4 percent. The problem with the official unemployment rate was that it had a downward bias as a result of the manpower training programs that were initiated by Johnson in his War on Poverty. Large numbers of young people were taking training courses for which no jobs were available to graduates. As a result, they easily signed up for another training course. By the time Nixon took over, close to a million people were involved in administering, teaching, and studying in these training programs.[1] It should also be recognized that Nixon inherited other social spending from Johnson's War on Poverty and that the increase in social spending generally in the Nixon years represented a postwar record.

Other factors differentiated the Vietnam War from earlier wars. In particular, there was a profits squeeze, so that no excess profits taxes were needed. The decline in capacity utilization rates indicated that there was still considerable slack in the system. The slowdown in labor productivity gains after 1966 was dramatic. Whereas the average rate of advance was about 3 percent between 1947 and 1966, the rate of increase dropped to 2 percent in 1967, and gains in productivity ceased altogether from about the middle of 1968 to the first quarter of 1970, according to Arthur Burns in his Pepperdine College speech of December 7, 1970. Burns recognized that the inflation "we are still experiencing is no longer due to excess demand. It rests rather on the upward push of costs, mainly sharply rising wage rates."[2] Even Republicans were now recognizing that there were two types of inflation, one that developed in an overheated economy (demand-pull) and the other (cost-push) that developed in an underheated economy.

President Nixon was committed to getting out of Vietnam, but not so fast as to produce a political backlash and accusations over "who lost Vietnam." As a result, real military expenditures fell in each of Nixon's six years in office. When the economy slipped into Nixon's first recession in late 1969, he was quick to admit that the reductions in military spending helped produce this result, rather than the "peace dividend" that naive peaceniks had assumed would be realized. By the time he would seek reelection in 1972, the cumulative budget deficit for the four years approached $90 billion, a new postwar record. The inflation rate peaked in December 1970, and unemployment also hit 6.1 percent, a level that persisted until the introduction of Nixon's New Economic Policy in August 1971. In contrast to the persistence of unemployment, however, there was a decline in the rate of increase in prices after December 1970, along with an anemic recovery from the first Nixon recession. Although he ran large actual deficits, Nixon insisted that his budget would be balanced if we had full employment.[3] On the basis of his failure to raise taxes to reduce the deficits, Nixon declared, "Now I am a Keynesian" in January 1971.[4]

With the next election only a little over a year away, Nixon and his economic advisers, Paul McCracken, the chairman of the CEA; future chairman Herbert Stein; Treasury Secretary John Connally with his assistant Paul Volcker; and Arthur Burns, now chairman of the Federal Reserve Board, retreated to Camp David in the middle of August, after which they announced the devaluation of the dollar and the outlines of Nixon's New Economic Policy. (See Appendix C for details.) The devaluation of the dollar (sometimes referred to as the "closing" of the gold window) represented a strong nation deliberately turning the terms of trade against itself. It was a classic example of exchange rate neomercantilism, a key characteristic of Bastard Keynesianism.

In addition to the devaluation, Nixon's New Economic Policy (NEP) abandoned the free market ideology that had underlain previous policy decisions. His frequent supporter, Milton Friedman, was appalled that Nixon had frozen wages and prices for three months, after which he planned to announce wage-price guideposts. The Democrats, including John Kenneth Galbraith, were also surprised that Nixon would take advantage of the powers that they never expected him to use.[5] Instead, the Democrats had planned to use his failure to impose wage and price controls as a campaign issue in 1972.

In addition, Nixon brought back an even more generous investment tax credit than the one he had eliminated after entering office. He also slapped a 10 percent duty on imports, aimed particularly at Japan, which was sluggish in accepting the necessity for a revaluation of the Japanese yen. By the time of the Smithsonian Agreement in December 1971, the Japanese surrendered, as the system of fixed rates of exchange was briefly patched together again, ending a three-month "float." Most currencies from the Third World, including the Yugoslav dinar, were devalued along with the dollar, thus indicating the real overall strength of the U.S. economy and its currency.[6]

There was really no economic basis for the devaluation since an article in the *Monthly Labor Review* of August 1971 showed that unit labor costs in the United States had been increasing less here than in the other G-7 countries. The devaluation represents a classic example of the use of the political business cycle, stimulating the economy before the election. Since the rate of price increase was already coming down, the wage and price controls were designed to disguise *expected* inflation, assumed by orthodox economists to arise from the devaluation of currencies.

With our new knowledge of the two types of inflation, however, we can see why devaluations tend to be especially inflationary. Typically, there is a trade-off between the two types of inflation—when one is up the other is down. Demand-pull inflation is predominant at 4 percent unemployment, while cost-push or supply-side inflation is all-important at 8 percent unemployment. As a result, our new Phillips curve has a more or less horizontal segment between 4 percent and 8 percent unemployment, reflecting this "trade-off."[7]

The real trade-off, however, was not between full employment and price stability. It was between demand-pull inflation plus growth, on the one hand, and cost-push or supply-side inflation plus stagnation, on the other. It is this feature that was later interpreted as a "crisis of the Phillips curve" in the mid- and late 1970s. Devaluations remove this trade-off or offsetting effect between the two types of inflation. We get demand-pull from the additional demand from abroad, at the same time that the costs of imported raw materials and imports generally will rise overnight.

The results of Nixon's New Economic Policy were superficially most impressive. By election time, the economy was growing very rapidly with minimum recorded inflation. Exports, especially of agricultural products, were booming, and real wages were rising at the fastest rate since 1966. At the end of the three-months price and wage freeze, Nixon's income policy was announced. (See Appendix D for a detailed evaluation.) Prices were projected to rise by 2½ percent per year, and money wages were to increase by no more than 5½ percent per year, with the difference representing an expected 3 percent historic increase in labor productivity. Administration of the new guidelines was under the leadership of the new CEA chairman, Herbert Stein, who personally had little sympathy for wage and price controls. Apparently, the whole plan represented a victory for John Connally and his assistant, Paul Volcker.[8]

Arthur Burns, as chairman of the Fed, was opposed to the closing of the gold window, according to Paul McCracken. Later he was accused of following too easy a monetary policy in 1972, an accusation that would seem to have little substance. The increase in the money supply seems to have been determined endogenously simply on the basis of the vigorous expansion taking place at the expense of the countries that had been forced to revalue their currencies as a result of the "Nixon Shock."[9]

In 1972, there was a crop failure in the USSR. As a result of the new détente, U.S. agriculture began selling our surpluses to the Soviet Union, rather than giving them abroad to the so-called Third World under Public Law 480. The devaluation also increased commercial sales of agricultural crops all over the world, especially to countries that had been forced to revalue their currencies. As a result, 1973 was a bumper year for U.S. agriculture, with farmers' incomes per capita approaching those of the urban population. These great agricultural successes prompted the Nixon administration to adopt a version of the Benson-Brannon program which had also been experimented with during the Eisenhower administration. U.S. farmers would henceforth grow as much as possible, rather than restrict their acreage in order to minimize agricultural surpluses.

During the last two years of the Nixon administration, the wage and price controls would be gradually phased out. But before this was completed in 1974, the OPEC countries engineered a huge increase in petroleum prices beginning in November 1973, thereby rectifying their worsening terms of trade after August 1971. Oil is typically valued in U.S. dollars in world markets as part of the dollarization frequently found in underdeveloped countries, so the United States' devaluation worsened OPEC countries' terms of trade, too.

This "oil shock" occurred at about the same time that the U.S. economy slipped into Nixon's second recession, which would eventually be labeled the "Great Recession." Because price increases were now double-digit—owing to the phasing out of the controls and the higher oil prices—it was not at first clear that there was a recession even taking place. It seemed inconceivable that both rapidly rising prices and rising unemployment could occur at the same time. This condition was labeled a "crisis in the Phillips curve." The expected trade-off between inflation and unemployment was not taking place, and there was increasing criticism of Bastard Keynesian demand management.

The Nonmilitary, Non-Keynesian Ford Interregnum

The accession of President Ford in August 1974 occurred when the unemployment rate was rising rapidly and there was double-digit inflation. Herbert Stein resigned along with Nixon at the end of August, and Alan Greenspan became the new head of the CEA. One of the new administration's first acts was to call a "summit meeting" on the economy, where leading economists testified for two days on the public broadcasting stations. The administration hoped that the top economists would recommend a tax increase to cool off an economy that featured double-digit inflation. "Whip Inflation Now" (WIN) buttons were used to reinforce the message.

Fortunately, sanity prevailed in the House of Representatives, where the late Al Ullman of Oregon, the chairman of the House Ways and Means Committee, worked up a plan to reduce tax rates that Ford reluctantly signed in March of the following year.[1] At the time, Ford admitted that he was changing his economic policy 180 degrees in the opposite direction. Almost immediately, the economy responded positively, but by then the Great Recession of 1973 to 1975 represented the sharpest decline in economic activity in the postwar period. The unemployment rate in 1975 was 8.3 percent, also a new record. As was to be expected, the combined passive budget deficit for the two Ford years, 1975 and 1976, was an unprecedented $125 billion. Republicans again were setting new records for deficit financing.

Eventually, some economists began to realize that OPEC had in effect levied a huge excise tax on the U.S. economy. Charles Schultze, who later became the chairman of President Carter's Council of Economic

Advisers, wrote an essay in 1975 arguing that the correct policy to counter the increase in an excise tax imposed from abroad was to decree a tax cut domestically.[2] Some states and countries outside OPEC also benefited from the price hike for oil. Texas, Wyoming, and Alaska were relatively immune to the effects of the Great Recession of 1973–75. Later Alaska would declare fiscal dividends or negative income tax payments for its residents from the huge increase in state taxes on its oil operations. Canada, which is self-sufficient in oil, was relatively unscathed, although some of the U.S. inflation spilled across the border.[3] Mexico and the USSR, which relied on oil exports for a large share of their foreign exchange, also prospered from OPEC's actions.

The world's bankers faced the problem of recycling the oversupply of "petrodollars" (which were in excess of OPEC countries' current developmental needs) by stepping up loans to Latin America and to Hungary and Poland in Eastern Europe. Since real interest rates during the decade averaged 0.3 percent, this seemed at the time to fit in with the interests of the developing countries, which were then growing rapidly. Later, in the 1980s, when real interest rates soared, the servicing or refinancing of these debts became so burdensome that they had to be written down in the case of Poland and Mexico. As a result, a significant amount of foreign investment in the '70s became in effect foreign aid in the '80s.

Economic thinking began to recognize aspects of supply-side inflation other than wages and oil prices. The environmental movement, which, to some extent, was initiated by Nixon on Earth Day, April 1970, began to attract the attention of legislators in the '70s and was responsible for increased amounts of what later came to be labeled "supply-side inflation" by Keynes's disciple Abba Lerner. Pollution was regarded as a good example of an external diseconomy with respect to the firm. One object of environmental legislation was to internalize these external diseconomies so that the costs of pollution would show up in the firm's balance sheets and be passed along to consumers of the polluting product in the form of higher prices.

In the international trade area, the fixed rates of exchange coming out of the Smithsonian Agreement came apart in 1973 and were superseded by a period of floating exchange rates. By January 1, 1979, however, the Western European countries decided to return to a partial system of fixed rates among themselves with the West German mark as the key currency. Thereafter the mark floated against the other major currencies of the world, while the franc and the lira lost their previous independence. Great Britain joined the Common Market in 1973, despite popular opinion that opposed this move. The British were forced to get a special dispensation to remain outside the European Monetary System, the pound continuing to float freely until after the departure of Thatcher in 1991, when Britain entered into the European Monetary System. For the remainder of the '70s, the dollar was chronically weak in comparison with other key currencies, and U.S. banks made huge windfall profits by selling dollars in exchange for stronger currencies. Typically, in their financial reports, banks listed the profits from currency speculation in foreign exchange separately, since they were so huge.[4]

This movement to floating rates of exchange represented a huge victory for Milton Friedman, who had blamed the so-called balance-of-payments problem of the United States on the system of fixed exchange rates supervised by the IMF. As mentioned previously, he sent a secret message to Nixon after his election advising this move. Although the IMF lost its raison d'être in the era of the floating exchange rates, it began to duplicate the work of and compete with the World Bank. As Friedman predicted, worry about the balance-of-payments problem declined or evaporated as the dollar floated downward. Despite the huge increase in oil prices, a surplus in the balance of trade occurred in 1975 during the Nixon-Ford Great Recession. A balance on current account surplus showed up by the end of the double-dip recession of 1980–82, and imports declined in 1982. It seems clear that recessions improve the foreign trade "problem" as perceived by conventional economists. Earlier this same thinking had underlain the stop-and-go policies pursued by the British government in the 1950s.

As the election approached in November 1976, the economy stopped its recovery or sputtered for three months. Ford refused to play the game of political business cycles—to apply stimulative monetary or fiscal policy—and was consequently defeated by Jimmy Carter, who no doubt also benefited from the electorate's reaction to Nixon's Watergate scandal and Ford's pardoning of Nixon.

Jimmy Carter, the Populist and Military Non-Keynesian

When Jimmy Carter was running for the presidency, he announced his economic goals: 2 percent unemployment, 2 percent inflation, and 2 percent nominal interest rates, or 0 percent real interest rates. His economic advisers, including Charles Schultze, chairman of the Carter CEA, pointed out that such populist goals were unrealistic. Nevertheless, Carter did appoint William Miller, an industrial capitalist from Textron, as head of the Fed, replacing Arthur Burns.[1] And it must be admitted that the real interest rate during the Carter years was very low. It had averaged between 1 percent and 2 percent in the 1950s and '60s, after the negative real interest rates of the '40s, but it was zero or even negative again during the Carter years, owing to the stepped-up rate of inflation.

During Carter's first year, Congress passed the Humphrey-Hawkins Bill, setting a goal of getting unemployment down to 4 percent, and requiring the CEA to make an annual calculation of the year in which this would be attained. For a few years, the CEA complied, but when the date of attainment of 4 percent unemployment became far in the future, publication was discontinued. It was also true that unemployment rates during the '70s were unusually high because of the baby boom, which had produced an inordinate number of teenagers, who are subject to very high unemployment rates. As a result of this phenomenon, the crude unemployment rates were frequently "age-adjusted," that is, the actual unemployment rates by cohort were weighted by a normal or standard year, such as 1956, rather than the actual percentages of the labor force in the current year. As a result, the age-adjusted unemployment rate was sometimes one percentage point lower than the crude or unadjusted unemployment rate.

Among the first acts of the new administration was to increase military spending as a result of U.S. pressure within NATO. Carter convinced each member of NATO in 1977 to agree on a 3 percent real annual increase in military spending until 1985. His own military budgets were in sharp contrast to the Nixon-Ford years, and he could legitimately boast when running for reelection that he was the largest military spender in peacetime. At the 1980 Democratic Party Convention in Detroit, Carter claimed that he had brought back the draft, a Freudian slip since he had only achieved the registration of potential draftees—as a first step. When leaving office in January 1981, he left a four-year military spending program that President Reagan barely fulfilled.[2] Thus, there was great continuity of military spending between Carter and Reagan, contrary to the rhetoric of the latter.[3]

Carter inherited an economy that was growing rapidly after the Great Recession of 1973–75, and the growth rate for his first three years was impressive. Carter's main problem stemmed from the second round of OPEC price hikes in 1979, which, in turn, reflected the political instability and decreased oil exports of Iran. Although Charles Schultze had understood in 1975 the need for reducing domestic taxes when another country or countries imposed what was, in effect, a huge excise tax, he treated the inflation as primarily of the demand-pull variety. In fact, like Nixon before him (but in contrast to President Ford), Carter and his advisers decided to play the political business-cycle game. They hoped to bring about a recession in the second half of 1979, which would allow time for a recovery before November 1980. Alas for them, the recession failed to show up and for a time it was dubbed the "peek-a-boo recession." (Now you see it, now you don't.)

In the fall of 1979, inflation (mostly supply-side coming from OPEC's second round) seemed to be getting out of hand in the eyes of the international bankers' IMF meeting in Belgrade, Yugoslavia. One of the U.S. participants, Paul Volcker, rushed back to take over the Fed, as Miller was kicked upstairs to become the secretary of the treasury. In effect, the international bankers had encouraged Volcker to "bite the bullet," a figure of speech popularized by both Friedrich von Hayek and Milton Friedman.

Early in 1980, Volcker stepped down hard on the monetary brakes, with policies that restricted consumers' credit (including giving up credit cards). The sharp drop in economic activity in the second quarter was the beginning of what was to become the first double-dip recession, the second and larger dip appearing in the early Reagan years. Although the first dip lasted only five months, it was impressive evidence of the power of the Fed in cooling off what appeared to be an overheated economy.

Chairman Volcker first announced that he was going to follow a "monetarist" policy long favored by Milton Friedman. He would look only at the increases in the money supply and attempt to regularize the increase. During this period when he ignored interest rates, they shot through the roof, producing the highest nominal interest rates of the twentieth century in the United States. Volcker let up a bit on the monetary brakes so that the economy was expanding in the third quarter of 1980. In his campaign for reelection, Carter differentiated his policy from Reagan's by saying that he would balance the budget *before* he would cut tax rates. Despite this one-quarter preelection growth in GNP, Carter was defeated, partly because of the impact of the high discomfort, or "misery," indexes (combination of the inflation and unemployment rates). When candidate Reagan asked his audiences whether they were better off today than they were four years earlier, many legitimately responded in the negative.

An active role in the economics of the Carter years was played by Alfred Kahn, his "price Czar." Kahn attempted to jawbone labor into accepting lower wage increases and played a big role in the deregulation of the airlines. The deregulation of the savings and loan banks was also begun in the late Carter years, although much of the misuse of their new power by the S&Ls occurred in the Reagan years. In deregulation and in military spending there was thus great continuity between the Carter and Reagan administrations.

During the late 1970s, there was great disillusionment with demand-managed Keynesianism and the beginning of supply-side economics. This theory developed on the editorial pages of the *Wall Street Journal*, under the aegis of Jude Wanniski.[4] In Congress, it showed up in the thinking behind the Kemp-Roth bill, calling for three successive annual tax cuts of 10 percent. By late 1980, George Gilder had produced his *Wealth and Poverty*, the New Testament of supply-side economics, which helped convince its most important convert, Ronald Reagan. Gilder argued that there was a need for greater inequality in the income distribution to provide the necessary savings for a higher rate of investment. Saving, in contrast to the investment stressed in Classical Keynesianism, was again the independent variable, as in neoclassical economics. In other words, the supply-siders claimed that it would be necessary to increase the savings rate before the investment boom could take place. The annual budget deficit, which had been reduced under Carter, should be lowered still more. The three successive tax cuts would lead to a balanced budget by 1984, in the same way that the 1964 tax cut seemingly almost led to a budget balance by 1965.

It was further asserted that the federal deficits "crowded out" invest-ment in the private sector. The Classical Keynesian argument of Alan Blinder, who would later be appointed deputy chairman of the Federal Reserve Board by President Clinton, on the other hand, was that a lower rate of saving would result in a "crowding in" of savings and invest-ment as newly reemployed factors of production raised incomes and activated presently unrealizable or disguised savings.[5]

The position of the Democrats under Carter reversed the "New Eco-nomics" of President Kennedy, whereas the tolerance of the deficit in the short run on the part of the Reagan administration represented a dramatic reversal in the economic policies of the two major political parties. The Democrats thereafter worried more about the deficits and proposed tax increases (especially at top levels) to bring them down. The Republicans under Reagan were, in effect, adopting a policy com-bining Military and Commercial Keynesianism more like that of John Kennedy. Thus, it is not surprising that Walter Heller was eventually invited to join a high-level Republican policymaking committee on international trade problems, much to the consternation of Martin Anderson, PEPAB's executive secretary and one of the early Republican supply-siders.[6]

Military Keynesian and Supply-Side President Ronald Reagan

President Reagan inherited an economy that was growing rapidly and continued to grow through the second quarter of 1981. Thereafter, for the next six quarters, there was a very sharp drop in the second half of the first double-dip recession. Fortunately, the three successive tax cuts sailed through Congress after the attempted assassination of Reagan in the spring of 1981. The first installment of 5 percent took effect on October 1, and the next two 10 percent annual cuts were to take place on July 1, 1982, and July 1, 1983. When the Reagan Recession began, his Chairman of the CEA, Murray Weidenbaum, pointed out that his (Keynesian) countercyclical economic policy was already in place. Military spending was booming and tax rates had just been cut.[1]

Still, the recession was at least as deep as the Great Recession of 1973–75 and the passive deficits set new records. Even after the recovery of the economy in 1983 and 1984, the relatively large deficits continued, contrary to the Reagan game plan. Reagan refused to raise tax rates (other than Social Security taxes) throughout this period, despite prodding from his Democratic critics, such as Carter's vice president, Walter Mondale, in the electoral campaign of 1984.

The Reagan recession produced double-digit unemployment for the first time since the Great Depression, and great pressures on labor to minimize their wage demands, in some cases resulting in wage givebacks. Union busting was also now fashionable, resulting in a sharp decline in the percentage of unionized workers in the labor force. The crude Phillips curve was working again as the rate of increase in inflation came down, partly due to new weaknesses in petroleum prices but also due to the disinflationary pressures of the growing buyer's market for labor.

The drop in the rate of wage and price increase was greater than the decline in nominal interest rates. As a result, real interest rates rose sharply to levels that hadn't been seen since the early years of the Great Depression. This very tight monetary policy of Chairman Volcker was vitiating the expected favorable results of the very easy fiscal policy and preventing the economy from getting back to full employment, when the federal budget would presumably be running a much smaller deficit and might even have been near balance. This monetary policy was justified by the Fed as an example of "leaning against the wind," a term that was first popularized by Fed chairman William McChesney Martin in the 1950s.[2]

President Reagan was helped superficially by the baby busters (those born after 1965), who were just beginning to enter the labor force. Compared to the upward bias of the crude unemployment rates of the 1970s, there was now a downward bias of the official or crude unemployment rate. In contrast to the early '70s, there was no effort on the part of government statisticians to age-adjust the unemployment data.[3] Since crime is also related to the supply of teenagers, there was a corresponding drop in crude or unadjusted crime rates, a development that Reagan was able to capitalize on, but that was more the result of the women's liberation movement and the introduction of the "pill" in the mid-1960s.

In contrast to the 1930s, when real interest rates were high but eventually came down, the Reagan years were characterized by continued high real interest rates. In the political debates before his reelection, Reagan would emphasize the decline in nominal interest rates but ignore the increases in real interest rates. As noted in the *Economic Report of the President, 1987*, the real long-term interest rate from 1982 to 1986 averaged 6.13 percent—about double the average over the past 130 years. The real rate of interest rose from an average of 0.8 percent from 1950 to 1980 to 4.7 percent from 1981 to 1990.[4]

These high real interest rates turned around the growing weakness of the dollar noted for the 1970s. Thus the United States became a preferred safe haven for hot money, and this produced great strength in the dollar until the Plaza Hotel Agreement of the G-5 countries (Canada and Italy were not invited since they had weak currencies) in 1985.[5] Because of this strong dollar, U.S. products became less competitive in world markets, and the balance-of-trade deficit grew. At the Plaza Hotel, it was decided that the five major powers would cooperate in bringing down the value of the dollar, which would eventually reduce the U.S. trade deficit. There were some similarities between this change and the devaluation of the dollar in August 1971, but since this was an era of (dirty) floating exchange rates, it was not a devaluation, but rather a cooperative depreciation of the dollar. Like the earlier case, however, it was an example of exchange rate neomercantilism.

In this early Reagan period, there was much talk about the so-called twin deficits: the budget deficit and the foreign trade deficit. Both deficits were in fact a reflection of the very high real interest rates. The budget deficit—as was the case for all record Republican deficits—was caused primarily by the growing underutilization of resources and the failure of the revenue side of the budget to grow. The balance-of-trade deficit was caused by the appreciation of the dollar due to the inflow of hot money that had tended to make U.S. products more expensive on world markets.

Reagan, to his credit, tended to play down the twin deficit problem by resisting any attempt to balance the budget by raising income taxes, an idea that the new chairman of the CEA, Martin Feldstein, began pushing in some of his speeches. Feldstein's "independence" very nearly caused Reagan to dissolve the CEA early in his second term.[6] As an alternative, Reagan finally appointed Beryl Sprinkel to the chairmanship, where he remained for the entire second term, although with a low profile.

At one of his press conferences, Reagan correctly recognized that the U.S. import surplus was actually a sign of the strength of the U.S. economy.[7] The United States was functioning as the "locomotive" for the entire advanced capitalist system, and our import surplus was a reflection of this role. U.S. growth was superior to Western European growth in the early 1980s, due largely to the bold fiscal policy—rapidly rising military spending and large budget deficits, in contrast to Western Europe (including Great Britain, which was actually raising taxes to help balance the budget). Margaret Thatcher imported a supply-side economist from the United States, but never really got the hang of Reaganomics.[8]

Early in the Reagan administration, the president described the USSR as an "evil Empire," but by the end of his first term, he had begun to modify his policy toward the Soviet Union. Although he more or less carried out the Carter four-year plan for military spending, increases in real military spending began to slow down during his second term. He began to push research for his potentially expensive "Star Wars" program, a "defensive" space weapon, even going so far as to promise to share the results of the successful fulfillment of this program with the Russians.[9]

At the same time that the U.S. economy was acting as the locomotive for the rest of the advanced capitalist system beginning in 1983, the

Soviet economy began to sputter. There were four bad crop years in a row, 1979 to 1982. The normal supply of new labor inputs virtually disappeared as a delayed result of a Soviet baby bust that also began in the mid-1960s, and the exhaustion of labor reserves from the now nearly complete mobilization of women and pensioners. Attempts to increase Soviet military expenditures to match the Carter-Reagan buildup were beginning to cut into what had still been increases in levels of living in the '70s. At this juncture, Mikhail Gorbachev arrived on the scene, with his program for "glasnost" (openness) and "perestroika" (restructuring).

The glasnost program was highly successful, with much pent-up criticism of the existing economic system now out in the open. Gorbachev was much less successful in restructuring the economy, which had come to a dead end with perhaps 25 percent of a much smaller Soviet GNP now being allocated to their military.[10] The Soviets had attained rough arms parity with the United States at the expense of significant increases in their current consumption. Soviet assistance to the Afghanistan government, as well as aid to Vietnam and Cuba, also drained the overcommitted Soviet economy. The Chernobyl disaster in April 1986 was another big setback, demoralizing Soviet leaders and jeopardizing public health in the area.

Gorbachev's economic advisers, particularly Abel Aganbegyan, compounded the problem by promising an acceleration (*uskoreniya*) of economic growth. As a result of a number of summit meetings between Reagan and Gorbachev (Geneva, Iceland, Washington, and Moscow), the USSR eventually capitulated. The military buildup of Truman, Kennedy, Johnson, Carter, and Reagan had finally been successful in winning the Cold War. The unification of the two Germanies on Western terms and the treatment of the East Germans as "losers" by West German capital was the best evidence of this fact.[11]

The monetarist economics of Milton Friedman also ran into trouble during the Reagan era. Measures of the velocity of money, which had increased regularly until 1980, became unstable, contrary to the assumptions of the quantity theory of money. Friedman himself was predicting a return to double-digit inflation by the end of 1984 on the basis of the large increase in the money supply in 1983. When the inflation rate at the end of 1984 was lower than it was at the beginning of the year, Friedman's stock began to decline. A decade later, Fed chairman Alan Greenspan would abandon changes in M-2 altogether as a reliable policymaking indicator.

Reagan's domestic policy in his second term concentrated on a bipartisan agreement to rationalize the tax system. Rather than a piecemeal approach, which would have most certainly been unsuccessful, it was proposed to include many little changes in a broad reform, labeled the

"Tax Reform Act of 1986." The investment tax credit or subsidy for investment was eliminated for the third time in its history. The capital gains tax rates were increased to pacify the Democrats, and income taxes reduced to only three tax brackets—16 percent, 28 percent, and 31 percent. The whole reform was intended to be "revenue neutral," which allowed Reagan to maintain correctly that he had not raised income taxes for eight years.

The payroll or Social Security taxes had been increased in 1983 as a result of the recommendation of a committee headed by Alan Greenspan and including Senator Pat Moynihan of New York. As a result of these huge regressive tax increases, the Social Security fund, which had been included in the general federal budget since the Johnson administration, was now beginning to show large surpluses that tended to minimize the consolidated federal deficit, which still exceeded $100 billion annually. Partly because of the sharp increases in real interest rates, the national debt, including servicing charges, rose rapidly, both absolutely and as a percentage of GNP. But it was still only less than half as large as the relative national debt in 1946.

Worry over the rising federal deficit produced the Gramm-Rudman-Hollings Law of 1985, which had wide bipartisan support. It set declining deficit targets over a five-year span, ending in 1991 with a supposedly balanced budget. If the deficit projected for a coming fiscal year exceeded the target by $10 billion or more, automatic across-the-board spending cuts (including military spending) were to go into effect. It also mandated that any new government spending must be explicitly financed by cuts in other types of spending or by "revenue enhancements."

In subsequent years, there have been several revisions, and the development of accounting tricks and revisions of targets, as the deficits mounted rather than decreased. Later, Senator Ernest Hollings, one of the original sponsors, would withdraw his support and call the entire deficit reduction process a sham. Senator Warren Rudman, another sponsor, would disgustedly resign his Senate post in 1992, becoming the codirector of the Concord Coalition with Paul Tsongas. Gramm-Rudman-Hollings joined the so-called ceiling on the national debt as a futile gesture of good intentions. The attention of the Republican Neanderthals (including George Bush) and Ross Perot next shifted in 1992 to proposing a "Balanced Budget Amendment" to the Constitution, which would in effect emasculate countercyclical fiscal policy for future administrations.

A minor problem in the Reagan years was the stock market break in October 1987, which followed the tightening of the discount rate by the new chairman of the Fed, Alan Greenspan. Although many pundits thought that it might be a significant break, the real GNP in the final quarter of the year grew at one of the most rapid rates in the long Reagan upswing: so much for the stock market as a reliable leading indicator. A similar experience, also precipitated by Alan Greenspan, would occur in the spring of 1994, as he began his seven-step program to double the federal funds rate from 3 percent to 6 percent.

By the time Reagan left office in January 1989, he could proudly look back at a long economic expansion beginning in early 1983 with an inflation rate of well below 5 percent. Labor productivity in manufacturing had inceased at an above-average rate for the postwar years, although overall productivity was still comparatively sluggish due to the crowding of white-collar workers and ex-manufacturing workers into the service sector, particularly into law, real estate, insurance, and finance. Profit rates recovered somewhat from their sluggishness beginning in 1966, partly as a result of the weakening of unionized labor, including the dissolution of the air controllers union (PATCO), which had originally supported Reagan in 1980. Real wages continued the decline that had begun after 1966 (with a brief uptick associated with the devaluation of the dollar and the consequent rapid growth of GNP of 1972–73) but family income stabilized as a result of increased female labor force participation rates. The average family was working harder (including a growing number of three-earner families) just to keep up with former living standards, as pointed out by Juliet Schor in her book, *The Overworked American*.

As planned by George Gilder et al., the distribution of income had become more unequal, with a meltdown of the middle classes. People at the top, particularly very high executives, were doing much better as a result of Reaganomics, but there was an increase in those who had dropped out of the labor force altogether, including an upsurge in homelessness and begging. The high real interest rates, which cut into the contruction of new homes, also reduced the used housing stock that typically passes on to the lower classes. Gini coefficients, derived from the Lorenz curve, which depict the change in the income distribution, rose as one measure of the increased inequality in the distribution of income. Although the upturn in Ginis actually began after the 1966–67 minirecession, the tempo of increases in inequality rose in the Reagan era.[12] Just as the full employment of World War II had produced greater equality, the growing slack of the economy after 1968 was producing greater inequality in the income distribution. The Reagan tax cuts, which favored the upper classes and savers, and the high real interest rates only exacerbated this problem.[13]

The administration attempted to explain the increased inequality as a byproduct of earlier home-leaving on the part of young people. Young offspring setting up their own apartments produced a decline in the size of the average family and an increase in the number of low-income family units. Another explanation for the increase in inequality was the institution of marriage and two-earner families. Divorce also tended to affect former wives' income relative to former husbands, particularly with the failure to pay child support. Overlooked as an explanation was the effect of affirmative action programs, which probably increased inequality within the ranks of both nonwhites and females generally.[14]

George Bush, Another Nonmilitary, Non-Keynesian President

When George Bush ran against Ronald Reagan in 1980, he described Reagan's supply-side economics as "voodoo economics." Although he presented himself to voters in 1988 as representing continuity with Reaganomics, his administration contained many warmed-up Ford advisers. Beryl Sprinkel was replaced by Michael Boskin, the first chairman of the CEA from west of the Mississippi. Boskin continued to fill this role with a low profile and by giving the usual positive twist to the unimpressive growth data.

Almost immediately after Bush's taking office, the economy slowed down so that the average growth in gross domestic product (which had replaced GNP as a measure of total product in 1991 at the urging of the United Nations) during his single term averaged about 1 percent per year. A recession showed up in the middle of 1990, but it was disguised for a time by the war in the Persian Gulf. Although the costs of this war were largely paid for by our allies, supplemented by a reduction in military inventories, the unemployment rate was no doubt held down by the use of military reserve units, who were now counted in the total labor force.

Before the Persian Gulf War, there was a compromise in the 1990 tax act designed to hold down government spending, and supposedly the rise in the budget deficit, which was moving in the opposite direction from that envisaged by Gramm-Rudman-Hollings. To achieve Democratic support, there was a small increase in taxes on upper income groups. It was this tax increase—as the economy began to sink into a recession—that angered supply-side economists, including Milton

Friedman, who correctly recognized that Bush was no longer a supply-side president, if he had ever been.[1]

Bush's advisers tended to blame the war for the recession and assumed that the ending of the war would be followed by resumed expansion. Although there was a brief upturn in economic activity after the war, the recovery was very weak and the economy very soon headed downward again, giving rise to the conclusion that we were having another double-dip recession.

Bush's address to Congress in January 1992 belatedly recognized that the United States was in a recession (since growth in the fourth quarter of 1991 was only 0.3 percent) and proposed a tax cut stimulus (including lower capital gains taxes amd the resurrection of the investment tax credit) with a deadline for Congress to submit a tax-cut proposal by March 20th. A compromise bill was worked out in Congress that included a lower capital gains tax, lower income taxes on the middle classes, and a slight increase in taxes on upper income groups, which incensed Bush. In contrast to the 1990 tax compromise, Bush angrily rejected the bill before he even received it, and the administration's opportunity to use the political business cycle before the upcoming election was largely missed.[2] A few leading indicators (and especially the stock market) were rising at the same time and Bush apparently decided to take a chance on an automatic cyclical recovery by election time in November. The Fed again moved to lower the federal funds rate supposedly to guarantee the continued expansion, rather than experiencing the first triple-dip recession.

Bush reaped the benefits of Gorbachev's surrender: the unification of Germany and the Velvet Revolutions of Eastern Europe. As a price of German unification, the Germans played a leading role in providing economic assistance to Eastern Europe and the former USSR. The Bundesbank was overruled to some extent by Chancellor Kohl in establishing the greater parity between the West and East German currencies. But eventually they administered the highest real interest rates in the advanced capitalist world, despite U.S. disapproval, and the fact that the German inflation rate was below the average inflation rate for the European Economic Community. Since the German mark was the key currency in the Common Market, the other members of the EEC suffered rising unemployment as a by-product of German ultratight monetary policy. By the spring of 1992, the entire advanced capitalist system, including Japan, appeared to be in the grip of a post–Cold War recession.

With the ending of the Cold War, there was a problem in providing some rationale for the continued spending of roughly $300 billion by the Pentagon. Their military strategists came up with seven possible areas of the world where future U.S. military interventions and expenditures might be needed in a "New World Order." Some reductions in military spending were planned, but usually several years in the future. In addition, the dismantling of nuclear weapons could be just as employment-creating as their installation had been. As the late Representative Les Aspin—later to become President Clinton's first secretary of defense—frankly admitted in early 1992, because of the unemployment connected with the second double-dip recession, it was inappropriate to consider serious reductions in the Pentagon budget at this time.

As the economy slipped into the second dip of a double-dip recession, the Council of Economic Advisers noted that "currently, real short-term interest rates are higher than they have been during many comparable periods in the past." The Canadian newsletter *Economic Reform* estimated that in 1990 the real short-term interest rate for the United States was 4.7 percent, compared to 10.9 percent in Canada, and 5.1 percent in both Germany and Japan.[3] Professor Benjamin M. Friedman of Harvard questioned the "aggressiveness" of the Fed, contending that there had been "little decline, and perhaps none at all, in the real interest rates that primarily matter for either stimulating or retarding business activity."[4] With President Bush rejecting the Democratic tax compromise in March, the tight-fisted Fed remained the only possible significant source of stimulus. And with Alan Greenspan still seeking bliss in zero inflation, the inevitable result was the election of Bill Clinton.

Can President Clinton Become a Nonmilitary Keynesian?

On the surface, it would seem that President Clinton might become the first out-of-the-closet nonmilitary Keynesian, now that Richard Nixon has apparently rejected this appellation. Clinton's more aggressive cutting of military spending as compared to his predecessor might augur well for the new president in 1993, provided other types of government spending (particularly public investment) are passed by Congress to offset the loss of these military-based jobs. Clinton's FY 1994 budget would increase the pace of reductions in active-duty military personnel in FY 1993 and FY 1994. His request would reduce active-duty end strength by 80,000 in FY 1993 and 108,000 in FY 1994 compared with the Bush budget, where the cuts were by 62,000 and 83,000, respectively.[1]

At the two-day summit in Little Rock before Clinton entered office, leading roles were played by James Tobin and Robert Solow, Nobel laureates influenced by a Keynesian philosophy.[2]

Both endorsed stimulus packages of between $50 billion and $60 billion to jump-start what seemed to be a relatively stagnant economy. Later, they coauthored a strong Op-Ed piece in *The New York Times*, timed to support Clinton's five-year budget plan to reduce the deficit by paring spending and raising tax rates. Nevertheless, they were "acutely aware that the weak and uncertain recovery—which this President inherited along with the deficit budgets—is not the best environment for the contractionary impulses that will inevitably come from spending cuts and tax increases."[3]

Clinton's appointment of Laura Tyson to chair the CEA would also seem to favor Keynesian policies, in view of her track record working with another Keynesian Nobel laureate, Lawrence Klein, on the Cuomo Commission on Competitiveness Report.[4] Her selection of Alan Blinder as a deputy, an economist who popularized (in an Economic Principles text coauthored with William Baumol) the concept of "crowding in" as opposed to "crowding out," was also encouraging. On the other hand, the Clinton Plan for reducing the budget deficit assumes that this will tend to reduce interest rates, implying that federal deficits have been "crowding out" funds that adversely affect savings and private investment. In contrast to Keynes after 1932, the Clintonites are still apparently treating savings as the dog and investment as the tail.

Between the election and inauguration, however, government statisticians reported that GDP growth in the third and fourth quarters of 1992 accelerated to nearly 5 percent. In addition, the so-called deficit problem inherited from Bush had turned out to be roughly $100 billion greater than previous estimates had indicated. Furthermore, the fact that Clinton had only received 43 percent of the vote and Perot had garnered 19 percent with his hard-line position on the budget deficit suggested the need for a cautious overall approach in Clinton's first economic proposals for stimulating the economy and creating jobs.

To appeal to the Perotistas, Clinton promised to reduce the deficit from more than 5 percent of GDP to something like 3 percent over five years. The seemingly rapid growth of GDP before he entered office allowed him to propose the tax increase on which he had campaigned: income tax increases for the upper 2 percent of the income recipients to rectify somewhat the inequities planned and carried out by the Reagan supply-siders. He proposed an energy tax designed to appeal to his environmental supporters. Clinton also attempted (without success) to revive the investment tax credit, which had been abandoned in the Tax Reform Bill of 1986, with special incentives for small businesses, which were expected to create the lion's share of jobs in the Clinton years. More direct employment creation was expected to come out of the relatively small $16 billion stimulus package, which included local projects for such public investment activities as swimming pools, summer jobs, and so on.

The stimulus bill had no trouble in the House of Representatives, but faced a filibuster by Senate Republicans led by Robert Dole. Clinton's program was denounced as full of "pork barrel" projects and as representing a return to Democratic "tax and spend" policies (as opposed to the more recent Republican "borrow and spend" policies). Despite the energy tax increases, which had also been called for by Perot's "shock therapy" approach, the Perotistas also criticized Clinton for spending too much. Clinton even offered to reduce his stimulus package but the Republicans didn't budge. Gridlock had appeared very early in the game.

On top of Clinton's problems with Congress and the Perotistas, the economic reports unexpectedly turned gloomy. There was no increase in jobs outside construction, unemployment was stuck at around 7 percent, the consumer confidence and the leading indicator indexes turned down, and GDP grew by only 0.7 percent in the first quarter of 1993. The Republicans tried to place the blame on the "unfriendliness" of the Clinton Plan to business, although most economists felt that the danger of a triple-dip recession was more the result of the economic policy left in place by the Bush administration. The acceleration of lower withholding taxes during the previous election year in a futile attempt to gain reelection had meant higher taxes and lower refunds in the new year.

On the monetary front, Alan Greenspan proposed to continue his search for "zero inflation" by setting targets for increases in the money supply that were lower than those of the previous year. By allowing himself to be photographed between Hillary Clinton and Tipper Gore, Greenspan hoped to cut off Senator Paul Sarbanes and his attempt to clip the wings of the Fed.[5]

The administration promised to finance more of its deficit by the sale of short-term bonds at lower interest charges and to reduce the sale of long-term bonds at higher interest rates, thereby lowering the charges for servicing the $4 trillion public debt inherited from the Reagan and Bush administrations. Long-term interest rates did come down a bit, and Clinton naively put his faith in further reductions based on his plans for a lower deficit.

In a preelection debate, Sander Vanocur raised the previously unmentionable question concerning monetary policy and the proper role of the Federal Reserve System. Of the three candidates' answers, Clinton came out more for a continuation of the Fed's policies than either of his opponents, Bush and Perot.

On the international trade front, the worldwide recession (outside of Greater China) has cut into our exports. Furthermore, the NAFTA agreement, which was supposed on balance to create jobs for the United States, was generating considerable division within the Democratic ranks, not to mention the solid opposition of Ross Perot.[6]

Clinton seems to be receptive to new ideas and willing to at least listen to people with Keynesian proposals. Whether he can educate and lead Congress should he become converted to a Keynesian philosophy is still an open question. Two of his role models are Franklin Delano Roosevelt and John F. Kennedy. The former had learned something from the "Roosevelt Recession" of 1937–38. FDR no longer was addicted to balancing the budget (which had helped bring on his recession), and by early 1939, he was describing increases in federal expenditures as "investments in the national economy."[7] However, it wasn't until World War II that he was converted into a Keynesian as a result of the necessity to defeat Hitler. President Kennedy was educated by Walter Heller to come out for unbalanced budgets in peacetime by the time of his June Commencement address at Yale University in 1962. As a populist, Clinton should be receptive to the idea that lower real interest rates can create jobs, bolster government budgetary revenues, and reduce the servicing charges on the national debt.

Like Reagan, Clinton created a long-range planning group, the National Economic Council headed by Robert Rubin, an experienced Wall Street operator. Under Reagan, the President's Economic Policy Advisory Board (PEPAB) was originally chaired by George Shultz, with Martin Anderson as executive secretary. Unlike the Council of Economic Advisers, which was more concerned with current economic policy, PEPAB was supposedly looking at long-range planning, or what President Bush would later describe derogatorily as that "vision thing." PEPAB's authority was briefly allowed to expire as a result of a decision by Donald Regan in 1985, and an attempt was made to bring Walter Heller into a top advisory board on international trade.[8] As a result of considerable adverse reaction from Milton Friedman, PEPAB was given a new lease on life, before being allowed to expire quietly with the beginning of the Bush administration. Judging by the Reagan experience, one wonders whether the National Economic Council will fare much better than PEPAB.

Conceivably there might be a useful role for the National Economic Council—one of reflecting on our economic history and explaining to the president and the public how the United States and the global economy generally has reached the current impasse. To understand our difficulties, it would be necessary to recognize that, outside of wars, there have only been three periods of sustained growth during the past seventy-five years:

1921–28 overall growth of 49 percent (GNP in 1958 prices)
1961–68 overall growth of 38 percent (GDP in 1987 prices)
1982–89 overall growth of 29 percent (GDP in 1987 prices)

These periods of "Seven Fat Years" corresponded to the Coolidge, Kennedy-Johnson, and Reagan years. Whereas part of the Johnson growth took place during the nasty little war in Vietnam (during which time the economy was underheated and subject to both a minirecession and then a full-blown recession), the Reagan years were also stimulated by the military buildup inherited from Jimmy Carter's four-year plan for the Pentagon disclosed in January 1981. I have also taken the liberty of assuming that Reagan's plan didn't go into effect immediately and that the first year of the Bush administration was really a reflection of supply-side economics, rather than the subsequent Bush relapse.

It is easy to see why Reagan was a great fan of Calvin Coolidge and immediately put up his picture on the wall of the Oval Office, according to Jeane Kirkpatrick. Ronald Reagan was the first economics major to become president, although his education was pre-Keynesian. It is frequently said that students who were educated before Keynes have never really understood Keynesian economics, and Reagan is an outstanding example of this phenomenon.

What do these three "Seven Fat Years" have in common, and in what ways do they differ? They were all years when investment was buoyant. In all of these expansions profits were stimulated and wages were compressed. The plowing back of profits into investment produced an investment binge followed by a capital hangover. In short, the high rates of investment produced a rapid increase in the capacity to produce goods, but final demand was inadequate to assure the full utilization of the new capacity.

In the Coolidge years, agriculture suffered from overproduction problems and failed to prosper along with the rest of the economy. The rates of wage inceases were lower than the inceases in labor productivity so that costs and prices, including the Consumer Price Index, fell gently.

In the Kennedy-Johnson years, the wage-price guidelines of 1962–66 permitted profits to receive a more-than-proportionate share of the rapid increases in labor productivity, as in the twenties. By the same token, labor received a less-than-proportionate share of the productivity growth.

In the Reagan years, the double-digit unemployment rates of 1982 produced a sharp decline in the rates of money wage increases (and further declines in real wages) as workers sought job security rather than the previous larger increases in money wages. The hostile attitude of the Reagan administration toward unions also helped produce somewhat of an upturn in profits from the depressed levels of the '70s.

Each of the "Seven Fat Years" was followed by economic difficulties. The Coolidge economy had very small defense or military expenditures, and the role of government spending as a built-in stabilizer was minimal. As a result, the decline in economic activity after 1929 during the Hoover administration was precipitous. What had been a mild disinflation turned into a sharp deflation from 1929 to 1932, which was only brought to an end by the New Deal public works projects.[9] At the time, it was obvious that the vaunted market was bankrupt and Keynes's *General Theory* in 1936 reflected this fact. It was only in the countries practicing a primitive Keynesian economics—Italy, Germany, and Japan—that the major economies recovered as a result of the abandonment of reliance on market forces. For the United States, it was only the growth of government spending during World War II that finally brought back full employment.[10]

In the Nixon years, there was great stagnation but at least the government budget was large enough to prevent any serious declines in economic activity. Nevertheless, the Nixon recession of 1969–70 was the first full-scale recession in the midst of a war, and the devaluation of the dollar in August 1971 presented the absurd example of the world's leading economy deliberately turning the terms of trade against itself in an attempt to beggar its neighbors, particularly Japan and West Germany. (See Appendix C.)

Likewise, the Bush administration experienced great stagnation after Reagan's "Seven Fat Years" despite what should have been the stimulating impact of the Persian Gulf military adventure. The average four-year annual growth rate for GDP was approximately 1 percent.

Another characteristic of all the "Seven Fat Years" was the cutting of tax rates. Reagan was particularly fond of citing the Coolidge tax-cutting experience. But the Reagan supply-siders—including Arthur Laffer—were also imitating the Kennedy administration's New Economics, particularly the stimuli to investment found in the investment tax credit of 1962 and accelerated depreciation. The Johnson administration's income tax cut in early 1964 and the resulting nearly balanced budget in 1965 was also a model for Reagan's claim that his budget would be balanced by 1984. The three Reagan tax cuts produced an investment binge, particularly in office buildings and shopping centers. The hangover following the tax reforms of 1986 was illustrated by the 20 percent vacancy rates in office buildings and the need for savings-and-loan bailouts of $200 billion.

During all three seven-year expansionary periods there was an increase in the inequality of the income distribution. The early Kennedy-Johnson years were initially an exception due to a greater commitment to full employment. But beginning around the minirecession of 1966–67, the measures of inequality (such as the Thiel coefficient) began to rise until 1972.[11] In the Reagan expansion, this increased inequality was actually a professed goal, as contained in George Gilder's *Wealth and Poverty*. It was assumed that the rate of savings would rise and that investment would follow. The Keynesian revolution, which contended that the rate of savings was too high, and that it was investment that determined savings (or that the investment dog was wagging the savings tail) had been repealed by the principles of Reaganomics.

Jack Kemp, who had presidential aspirations for 1996, claims to be a great believer in the fact that we should learn from our history. My reading of all three supply-side expansions is that they appear to work in the short or medium run, but that they create long-term problems such as those we are facing at the present time. In our type of economic system, there should be some proportionality between investment and consumption. If investment outruns the consumption possibilities— which are determined by the changes in income distribution toward greater equality—there develops what Marx would call a "realization problem." Marx and orthodox Marxism may in fact be dead, but the realization problem remains.[12]

In comparing the aftereffects of the three investment binges, we can vividly see the new stabilizing role of government expenditures in the post–World War II years. Before 1929, it was possible to draw an analogy between family, state, and national budgets. If families had to balance their budgets, so too must the states and the federal government.[13]

The most important lesson to be learned from the Great Depression, the writing of Keynes, and the World War II experience is that the federal government now has an important responsibility for preventing another Great Depression, namely, fiscal policy or the spending and taxing involved in the annual national budget. The federal budget provides stabilization and the possibility of stimulating growth, *provided* it receives the cooperation of those in charge of monetary policy, rather than a policy of "leaning against the wind."

One of Keynes's strong beliefs was that the international gold standard before World War I had a strong deflationary bias, something that was also recognized by William Jennings Bryan at the turn of the century. Even attempts to patch up the gold standard by Great Britain after World War I produced a deflationary bias, particularly in England, which did not share in the postwar prosperity found in other countries, especially the United States, Canada, and Germany, after 1923. In the interwar period, Keynes "constantly stressed the point that the burden of adjustment should primarily be assumed by the surplus countries."[14]

As a result of the Russian Revolution in 1917, the USSR became the first country to reduce significantly the role of international bankers. Later, in the 1930s, the fascist powers reduced the influence of bankers and their tight monetary policy. And even Roosevelt, in the interest of defeating Hitler, put monetary policy on hold for the duration. Furthermore, after World War II, the demonetization of economies spread to

Eastern Europe, China, North Korea, Cuba, and Vietnam with negative real interest rates the rule.[15]

As World War II was being successfully concluded, the Allies, including the USSR, met in Bretton Woods to draw up plans for the postwar international monetary system. Both Keynes and Harry Dexter White, who led the U.S. delegation, were anxious to reduce the prewar power of the international banking community. As a result, it was decided to adopt fixed, rather than fluctuating, rates of exchange supervised by the International Monetary Fund. "Countries with short-run temporary imbalances were to be helped over the hump by the IMF rather than be forced to apply self-flagellation" (as with the gold standard).[16] This idea was sold to policymakers as necessary to reduce the risks associated with international trade resulting from the need to repatriate profits earned from foreign investment.

The results were highly positive for twenty-five years, with foreign trade rising at roughly twice the rates of gross domestic products. The problem was that there was a bias in favor of devaluations and no, or little, pressure on countries to revalue their currencies if they were running trade surpluses. If devaluations were approved by the IMF, they were accompanied by austerity programs designed to reduce the role of government, end deficit financing, and remove subsidies to consumers. All were designed to cool off overheated economies and were nearly as deflationary as the earlier international gold standard had been. Since the devaluation of the dollar and the period of the "dirty float," there has been a deterioration in the "propensity to trade" and instability of the rate of growth in world trade. The completion of the Uruguay Round of the General Agreement on Trade and Tariffs was delayed by growing protectionism on the part of the Common Market. Individual countries within the European Community are turning inward and the European Rate Mechanism is breaking down owing to the obstinacy of the Bundesbank. In the heartland of pre-Keynesianism, they have been insisting on the use of an overall tight monetary policy to treat a unified Germany, one part of which is decidedly underheated.[17]

The Unraveling of Classical Keynesian Economics in the United States over the Past Half-Century

MONETARY POLICY

In the postwar years, we have seen the rise in real interest rates from −8 to +6 percent or by approximately 14 percentage points. The key victories in bringing monetary policy back to its position before Keynes's *General Theory* were the Treasury Accord of 1951 and Paul Volcker's accession to chairmanship of the Fed in 1979. His successor, Alan Greenspan, has been even more doctrinaire in suggesting that our ultimate goal should be "zero inflation."

The zero inflation movement is certainly not confined to the United States. The former Bank of Canada governor, John Crow, after his apprenticeship with the International Monetary Fund, was anxious to constitutionalize this goal, despite the fact that Canada's unemployment rates have typically been 3 to 4 percentage points higher than ours in recent years. New Zealand has actually put "zero inflation" into its most recent constitution. And, according to *Economic Reform*, the lively monthly of the Committee on Monetary and Economic Reform, "it was by the grace of God rather than of Brian Mulroney that Canadians at the last moment, managed to keep it out of theirs." At one point, the United States pressured the Japanese Central Bank to raise its discount rate so that the Fed could postpone dropping its own.[1]

The strategies for achieving zero inflation are laid out by the Bank for International Settlements at Basle, Switzerland. This bank was created in 1930 to facilitate the payment of German reparations and the borrowing under the Dawes and Young Plans that enabled the Germans to go through the motions of paying reparations after World War I. The BIS was composed of central bankers (except in the United States, where a central banking group, including J.P. Morgan, participated), rather than governments. It very nearly went out of existence after World War II, partly because of its supposed cooperation with Nazi Germany during the war. Resolution V of the Bretton Woods Agreement in 1944, following an initiative by Norwegian expatriates, called for its replacement by the International Monetary Fund. Although its activities are somewhat mysterious, it is a center of the belief that gold must be the basis for a sound currency.[2] In this respect, they are second cousins of the gnomes of Zurich.

Switzerland, incidentally, is probably the only country in the world to have experienced less inflation than the United States since World War II. Whenever unemployment developed, as it did during the worldwide Great Recession of 1973 to 1975, the Swiss resolved this problem simply by sending home their "guest workers," both foreigners and women. It was one of the three German-speaking countries that experienced uniquely declining female labor force participation rates between 1975 and 1985, the United Nations "decade of women," the others being West Germany and Austria.[3]

The chronic policy of the Fed seems to be summarized by movements that "cool off an overheated economy." Any uptick in the Consumer Price Index (which Alan Greenspan now admits is subject to a serious upward bias) can be used to justify an increase in interest rates or a refusal to lower them. There is a general assumption on the part of monetary authorities that some rough Phillips curve exists, whereby the cure for inflation is to increase deliberately the amount of unemployment. Even Sweden decided in 1991 that it should consciously raise its low unemployment rates to reduce the rate of inflation, which had been higher than that found in EEC countries; Sweden had hoped to join the EEC after Maastricht.[4]

As mentioned previously, there is an upward bias in our measures of inflation. The results—using a Laspeyres index—show what it would have cost to buy a certain market basket of goods and services in an earlier year.[5] The problem is that people don't continue consuming the earlier market basket: they tend to substitute things that decline in price or go up more slowly than average for those products whose prices rise faster than average. There is also little attention paid by the Bureau of Labor Statistics to sales or growth of discount centers, coupons, tie-in promotions ("free" glasses of wine or food and shelter for children), and the growth of the underground economy where consumers and producers of services share the tax benefits that would have gone to the federal government.[6]

Just as our offical statistics exaggerate the rate of inflation, they also underestimate the amount of unemployment for both labor and capital. There was a measure of unemployment (U-7) that took into account "discouraged workers" or part-time workers, who would like to work full-time, but it has been scarcely publicized since it was about 1.5 times as large as the official unemployment rate. As of January 1994, the Bureau of Labor Statistics has discontinued the calculation of U-7. Recent studies by James Medoff of Harvard University emphasize the decline in the quality of jobs obtainable. The number of self-created jobs as "consultants" also disguises the real unemployment rate.

Unemployment of capital—the capacity utilization rate—is minimized by the Federal Reserve Board, which deliberately writes off capacity at frequent intervals. In the 1960s, this index was the province of McGraw-Hill and was more reliable. All of these statistical biases reinforce the need for tighter monetary policy.

FISCAL POLICY

Both political parties recognize the trade-off between the inflation and unemployment problems depicted by the conventional Phillips curve. But the Republicans tend to worry more about the inflation problem and its erosion of capital values, while the Democrats, in view of their traditional support by organized labor, have tended to pay more attention to the unemployment problem.

Because of these biases, the Republicans have presided over record highs in the real budget deficit—Eisenhower (1959); Nixon (1971–72); Ford (1975–76); Reagan (1982–83); and Bush (1992). These record deficits do not come from the spending side; rather, they arise primarily from the revenue side of the budget. It is the failure of an increasingly underheated economy to pay taxes and the typical willingness of Congress to pay extended unemployment compensation that accounts for the so-called deficit problem.

As the late Walter Heller recognized, these large passive deficits have very little to do with inflation. The Reagan experience shows, on the contrary, that higher passive deficits have been associated with a taming of inflation. Increased spending, even for the military, would have produced smaller deficits were it not for the very tight monetary policy administered by the independent Fed. The high real interest rates engineered by Volcker also exacerbated the budget deficit and growth of the national debt in the 1980s. By fiscal 1993, the interest charges alone accounted for three-fourths of the budget deficit.

Keynes made no distinction between military and nonmilitary spending, nor did he prefer the cutting of taxes to increased government spending in overall fiscal policy. Bastard Keynesians in the United States have assumed that a bias toward cutting taxes will minimize the growth of the public sector, something that is more acceptable to Republicans particularly. And if you must have a public spending sector it can only be legitimized by either military spending or nonmilitary spending under the guise of military spending.[7]

THE NATURE OF INFLATION

Our thinking about inflation has changed greatly during the past half-century, something that could not have been foreseen by Keynes. Lord Keynes recognized the stickiness of wages and urged tax increases in a fully employed wartime economy. But he left no guidelines on how to handle supply-side inflation in an underheated economy, since this has been a relatively recent development, roughly since 1966.

In the early postwar years, it was assumed that there was only one type of inflation, the variety that occurred in wartime when "too much money was chasing too few goods." It can now be labeled "demand-pull inflation," although there is little evidence that any significant amount remains in 1995. There is no serious shortage of any good or service, nor is there any evidence of too much money in the system. In fact, the *real* supply of money has grown more slowly than the *real* total product, thanks to the persistently tight monetary policy of the Fed.[8]

The inflation still showing up in the offical price indexes can best be described as "supply-side inflation," to use a term coined by the late Abba Lerner.[9] Although wage-push inflation could be an element of supply-side inflation if we ever got back to genuine full employment, there has been a great weakness in money wage increases (and decline in real wages) in the Reagan-Bush-Clinton years. Thus, current supply-side inflation comes from costs other than wage increases that exceed the growth of productivity: environmental cleanup costs, exise and other sales taxes (including two rounds of OPEC "taxes" in 1973 and 1979 and the Clinton gasoline tax after 1993), distribution costs (advertising), and most importantly, the high real interest rates that are overhead costs imperfectly spread over less output than would be the case if our capacity utilization rates were higher. The high real interest rates might be an appropriate policy if we faced a demand-pull inflation and full employment. But when applied to supply-side inflation in an underheated economy, they simply worsen the problem.

INTERNATIONAL ECONOMIC RELATIONS

Operating in the midst of the Great Depression, Keynes did little theorizing about international trade. His highest priorities were nationalist rather than internationalist, and he was also something of a protectionist. Although he approved of the devaluation of the British pound in 1931, this was not a solution for all countries since in the long run exports and imports are a zero-sum game. My exports are your imports and vice versa. In other words, exports and imports are two sides of the same coin. The folly of "beggar-thy-neighbor" policies was evident in the 1930s. Keynes was too smart not to agree with Adam Smith's nonmercantilist conclusion that the fruits or benefits of international trade for the economy as a whole—as opposed to individual businessmen—were imports rather than exports, which were the costs.

Nevertheless, Keynes confounded his colleagues by adopting a rather positive view of the mercantilists and rejected the theory of free trade in the midst of the Great Depression. According to Joan Robinson, "when Keynes attacked the dominant orthodoxy, one of the things that grieved my teachers most was that he should try to rehabilitate the mercantilists, thus damaging the claim of the free traders to superior benevolence and wisdom."[10]

Bastard Keynesianism sees nothing wrong with using the foreign trade or aid sector as another employment-creating institution. It is always better to pay reparations than receive them, assuming that your capital is intact after the war, as was the case for both Canada and the United States. Thus both countries made no attempt to get reparations from the defeated powers, Germany and Japan. Instead, the Cold War provided an excuse to develop the U.S. Marshall Plan, which gave over $13 billion worth of goods and services to rebuild Western Europe as a bastion of anti-Communism. Some of the U.S. prosperity generated by the Marshall Plan may have spilled over into Canada. Canada was also involved in the Korean War. Nevertheless, Canadian growth in the last half of the 1950s was the slowest of the G-7 countries. See Appendix E for a discussion of Canadian Keynesianism.

No attempt was made to obtain reparations from Japan, nor were the Japanese recipients of Marshall Plan assistance. Conventional wisdom holds that U.S. orders for the Korean War helped jump-start the Japanese economic miracle, but the problem at the time was hardly a lack of demand since the war had turned the Japanese economy into a supply-side nineteenth-century model with many of Japan's cities in ruins. Later, the United States would pressure Japan to pay employment-creating reparations to less-developed countries in Asia that had been occupied by Japanese troops in the 1930s and early '40s. An exception was Communist China, which has never been indemnified for the terrible destruction inflicted by Japanese troops. Mao, in fact, refused reparations in 1972 since he was dogmatic in his belief in "balanced equivalents" or balanced trade with each trading country.[11] The acceptance of reparations would, in his eyes, correctly require an import surplus. It is also significant that Henry Kissinger had no problems with a promise of $3 billion in reparations for postwar Vietnam.

Japan, like all advanced capitalist countries, recognizes the employment-creating effect of a foreign aid program. It has one of the largest aid programs and has surpassed the United States in giving to the Philippines, for example. Canada, like the United States, came out of the war with its capital unscathed. Its economy was slightly less involved in the Korean War and foreign aid generally in the early postwar years. Unlike other countries, however, Canada maintained a floating currency during the 1950s. During this period, the Canadian dollar floated upward and eventually became more valuable than the U.S. dollar in the late 1950s. As a result of the relative lack of militay spending after the Korean War, less foreign aid, and the strong floating currency, Canada was forced to devalue in 1962 (92.5 Canadian cents to the U.S. dollar) and joined other currencies whose value was fixed by the International Monetary Fund. This experience was roughly ten years before Nixon's use of devaluation to stimulate U.S. economic growth and assure his reelection.

In recent years, Canada has developed a significant foreign aid program, one that is three times more important relative to GNP than the U.S. program. Although the growth of nuclear power has been stagnating domestically, Canada has given a nuclear power plant, which went onstream in 1995, to Romania. Canada was also an early trader with and recognizer of Communist China, long before Nixon achieved détente in 1972, and even today contributes foreign aid to China, in contrast to the United States. Unlike the United States, Canada has also maintained relatively friendly relations with Cuba, and Canadian citizens are able to enjoy their winter vacations in sunny Cuba.

The U.S. foreign aid program, including both military and nonmilitary assistance, has become an important employment-creating institution, costing annually over $16 billion in new appropriations currently. Politicians worry about adverse voter reaction to increased foreign aid, but Bastard Keynesians recognize the costless nature of such gifts when financed out of resources that would otherwise be unemployed. Politicians worry about finding the foreign aid dollars to underwrite the Polish or Yeltsin "shock therapy" programs, but never fear, there is always some slush fund or aid previously appropriated that can provide the wherewithal.[12]

An interesting attempt was made by early Reagan supply-siders to phase out the Export-Import Bank, which is a subsidy for U.S. exports paid for by U.S. taxpayers. Its origins go back to 1934 when it was created to finance loans to the newly recognized USSR.[13] But it really developed after World War II. Supply-side economics is nineteenth-century economics when foreign aid is unthinkable or unnecessary. This conflict between nineteenth-century supply-side economics and Bastard Keynesianism was decided finally in the 1980s in favor of the latter twentieth-century institution, and the Export-Import Bank lives on![14]

BASTARD KEYNESIANISM AND SUPPLY-SIDE ECONOMICS

Despite the uneasy marriage between Bastard Keynesianism and supply-side economics, it must be admitted that the two most rapid growth periods after World War II were the Kennedy-Johnson and Reagan administrations when both ideologies flourished side by side. Although both positive experiences were impressive in the short run or medium run (six or seven "fat" years), they both eventually ran into long-term troubles. Both the Nixon and Bush administrations were saddled with the long-term consequences of the offspring of this unholy marriage. In both cases, there was a capital hangover following an investment binge. In the words of Paul Krugman, "It is possible to make the case that the weakness of the economy after 1990 was at least part due to the legacies of Reaganomics."[15]

The same can be said for the Harding-Coolidge years, 1921–28. As in the later Kennedy-Johnson and Reagan years, there was a movement toward greater inequality in the distribution of income. Unlike the later "Seven Fat Years," however, there was no significant government sector to stabilize the economy and the Great Depression ensued.

An artificial underwriting of investment through subsidies such as the investment tax credit or rapid depreciation allowances eventually produces a poor capacity utilization rate. This can be seen clearly in the results of the investment subsidies for the construction of office buildings from 1981 to 1986. By 1992, there was still an office occupancy rate of only 80 percent and pressure on the Bush administration from the real estate industry to subsidize the losses resulting from underutilization, which the original subsidies made possible.

One wonders if some of the sluggishness in measured productivity might not itself be the result of the investment binge. There are three possible measures of productivity: labor productivity, capital productivity, and so-called factor or multifactor productivity where both labor and capital are in the denominator.[16] Typically we measure labor productivity with only the labor inputs in the denominator since the data are more readily available and reliable. But when we measure changes in labor productivity we are also measuring changes in capital productivity, since higher labor productivity usually involves additional capital per worker. The artificial scrapping of perfectly useful machinery—or the proliferation of capital as in Automatic Teller Machines, telephones on planes, or brain scanners—doesn't help improve labor productivity as conventionally measured. However, the artificial scrapping of capital—as a result of rapid depreciation and the investment tax credit—does bring down the cost of steel scrap, a major raw material input in steel production. We are now exporting 8 percent of our steel output as a result of our comparative advantage in steel scrap, which emanates from the investment subsidies.

An attempt to stimulate investment artificially might have made some sense in the years of the Cold War. One of the advantages of military spending was that it weakened the pre–Great Depression intimate relationship between investment and consumption. Investment could be accelerated as long as the military industrial complex assured the consumption power (through the relatively higher wages and salaries of its workers) to absorb the output of the consumer goods sector.

In the 1920s, the free play of market forces eventually produced an imbalance between the capacity to produce goods and the ability to absorb the output of this vastly increased capacity. The advanced capitalist system in the United States is still faced with this same problem; the recent relative declines in labor and farm incomes in the 1980s and '90s, as in the '20s, do not bode well for the future rational development of the system. The agenda of the Gingrich Republicans to wipe out the welfare state would only intensify the problem.

Conventional economics, both Republican and Democratic, assumes the need for increased investment to restore the competitive position of the United States in world markets. One problem with this position is that there is so little statistical evidence supporting this lack of competitiveness.[17] Certainly there are great needs for government investment in our decaying infrastructure. But in view of the already profligate use of the planet's resources by the United States, shouldn't we begin advocating "sustainable investment" as a basis for sustainable growth rather than subsidized investment for God knows what?

Where Do We Go From Here?

Both Republican and Democratic economic policies in the United States have reached a dead end or, as Joan Robinson would say, an "awkward corner." Bastard Keynesianism and supply-side economics have produced an economy that seems to represent what Joseph Schumpeter was predicting in the early 1940s in his *Capitalism, Socialism and Democracy*. At that time, he felt that Keynesian economics could stabilize the system, but that in the process, capitalism would lose its dynamism. If we take the advanced capitalist system as a whole, growth since World War II has averaged a lower percentage in each successive decade, and we can predict that the 1990s will be no exception.

One key toward understanding what is wrong with economic policy is found in understanding the role of the real rate of interest. Paul Volcker winces when Helmut Schmidt complains bitterly about "the highest real interest rate since the birth of Christ."[1] It was particularly hard for him to take since Volcker was heavily influenced by a Hamburg stopover in 1979 on his way back from the IMF Conference in Belgrade, Yugoslavia. Schmidt and the president of the Bundesbank, Otmar Emminger, apparently played an important role in encouraging Volcker to tame inflation by "biting the bullet."

Actually, the average real interest rate for the 1930s was higher than it was in the 1980s. It averaged 6.01 percent in the 1930s (1930–39) and only 4.69 percent in the 1980s (1980–89).[2] The real interest rate was particularly high in the early 1930s as deflation reduced prices generally much faster than nominal interest rates. The real interest rate peaked at 12 percent in 1932 but was negligible for the latter half of that decade.

Thus, it is more correct to emphasize the *longest* period of high real interest in the 1980s and '90s.

On the one hand, these high real interest rates have a positive side—higher real incomes for recipients. Senior citizens, for example, frequently depend on interest and this is one group of citizens who still had declining poverty rates in the 1980s. Since interest tends to be paid more by those at the bottom of the income ladder (for example, high installment credit charges) and received from bonds by those who are already nearer the top, the high real interest rate helps explain the acceleration of Gini coefficients measuring increased inequality in the income distribution in the 1980s and '90s. Thus, Alan Greenspan may have more power over these developments than he cares to admit.[3] It—along with the upward bias of the Consumer Price Index—also explains the atypical decline in the percentage of seniors living below the poverty line.

Those who are hurt by high real interest rates include debtors, especially underdeveloped countries and domestic farmers. The recycling of petrodollars in the 1970s was very attractive for Third World countries in view of the negligible real interest rates in that decade. Likewise, U.S. farmers tended to borrow for additional land as a result of higher incomes emanating from Nixon's devaluation of the dollar and the favorable low real interest rates in the 1970s.[4] Both underdeveloped countries and farmers have been hard pressed to service and refinance the earlier loans in the 1980s and '90s as a result of the sudden jump in the real interest rates.

In my view, it will take a great change in our thinking to revert to Classical Keynesian solutions. Briefly, it will require a rejection of the three Ms: monetarism, militarism, and mercantilism. Supply-siders and monetarists will have to recognize that nineteenth-century economics is no longer appropriate as we approach the twenty-first century. Bastard Keynesians will be forced to realize that in practice the neoclassical synthesis has fallen apart. We have been irrationally practicing "employment saving" at the microeconomic level and "employment creation" at the macroeconomic level. As a result, we are comparatively efficient in managing our factories at the same time that we increasingly waste resources at the macroeconomic level.

Macroeconomic policies are typically judged on the basis of whether jobs are created, never on the basis of whether any utility or satisfaction is obtained from the job and the products or services at the end of the line. This can be illustrated by the reaction of the political system to such rational nineteenth-century Friedmanian ideas as the "negative income tax" or a "flat tax without the long form." In the Nixon years, experiments were made in a number of communities of the effects on work incentives of the negative income tax—the payment of cash to the poverty-stricken. The results frequently showed a greater motivation to work as a result of cash payments from the government to the poor. The problem was that too many jobs would be lost in administering welfare if this simple procedure of paying money to poor people were used. The so-called earned income tax credit introduced under President Ford and expanded under President Clinton represents a version of the negative income tax. Ironically, the Gingrich Republicans seem to want a cutback in these Friedmanian payments.

The same supply-side reasoning can be applied to the flat tax without the long form, as espoused most recently by Governor Jerry Brown in 1992, Representative Dick Armey of Texas in 1995, and Presidential aspirant Steve Forbes in 1996. Too many jobs would be lost among accountants, tax experts, and the Internal Revenue Service itself to permit the introduction of this rational tax scheme.

Assuming that we recognize the negative role of the high real interest rates in the 1980s, we are still faced with the problem of distinguishing between cause and effect, one of the principal problems in economics. The conventional view is that the huge deficits have forced the Fed "to lean against the wind." The very easy fiscal policy under Reagan supposedly brought about a very tight monetary policy.

The revisionist Classical Keynesian view holds that the real interest rates resulted from conscious Fed decisions to "bite the bullet" in late 1979 when the budget deficit under President Carter was minimal. The high real interest rate thus represents the causal variable, and the larger deficits—coming from an underheated economy—are the effect of this very important policy change.

The idea of leaning against the wind—that fiscal and monetary policy should move in opposite directions—seems to be at the root of the problem. The Fed, whose members seldom face unemployment, continually views inflation as the prime culprit and has acted accordingly. As a long-term result of this policy, we have licked inflation and the economy is now poised on the brink of deflation.[5] Among countries already showing signs of deflation are Japan (where it is labeled "price destruction"), Canada, and Argentina. As for healthy growth prospects, the world economy appears to be dead in the water.

The fear of federal government deficits and the national debt resulting therefrom could also use a bit of demystification. As Robert Heilbroner and Robert Eisner have frequently pointed out, it is high time that expenditures by the federal government that represent "investment" should be separated out in a capital budget, just as we ordinarily do in local budgeting. A case can also be made for excluding the Social Security trust fund from the Federal Budget.[6] As experience shows, the

S&L bailouts and the Persian Gulf War—and any other one-time-only expenditures—can be financed in the short run on an "off-budget" basis.

As long as unemployed resources exist, we should be relatively cavalier about any remaining deficits that are required to put labor and capital back to work, after which they will contribute additional tax revenue. Once the principle of functional finance or monetization of the debt is recognized as applicable to a nonwar economy, the Fed can be instructed chronically to buy government long-term bonds leading to lower long-term real interest rates. In recent years, the Fed has been monetizing about 10 percent of the growth in the national debt, although it is reluctant to do so.

The present gap between the high long-term and the low short-term interest rates is frequently deplored. It is the opposite of the "operation twist" attempted by the Kennedy-Johnson economic advisers. At that time, the Fed tried (without success) to keep down long-term interest at the same time that high short-term interest would attract "hot money" and balance our capital accounts. Presumably the Fed should be able to eliminate the differential today by constantly purchasing long-term bonds on the open market once it is so instructed, as in early 1942.

As for the national debt itself, it should be emphasized that a large part of this debt is held by U.S. citizens, presumably more affluent risk-avoiders. As societies become more mature and affluent, we might expect this category of citizens to grow. Hence, the need is for a larger national debt to accommodate these risk-avoiders. As for the next "thirteenth" generation—over which copious crocodile tears are shed by the Concord Coalition (Pete Peterson, Paul Tsongas, and Warren Rudman)—presumably the descendants of current bond holders will inherit these assets and continue to receive interest on the bonds, hopefully at lower real interest rates.

One of the interesting characteristics of U.S. politics is the lack of criticism of the Fed and monetary policy generally, as has been noted in the Bush-Clinton-Perot preelection debate. Apparently there is a bipartisan agreement not to discuss appropriate monetary policy. The Fed is supposedly "independent," although it is frequently subject to a certain amount of jawboning by the president. The chairman of the Fed, particularly Paul Volcker and now Alan Greenspan, has been treated as a "sacred cow" far removed from criticism. In my view, bankers should be treated as the special interest group they are. They do have a special interest in fighting inflation since they are required to keep reserves that are not subject to earning interest, and with inflation, these sterile reserves must be constantly replenished. On the other hand, bankers as a group are not ordinarily affected by unemployment. But their self-centered policies should not be a burden to the rest of society. President Woodrow Wilson explicitly declared that control of the banking system must be "public, not private, must be vested in the government itself so that banks must be the instruments, not the masters of business."[7]

MILITARISM

How are we to deal with the dependence of the U.S. economy on military spending? First, it must be recognized that in the years of the Cold War we have had an irregular growth in such spending. In the years when military spending was growing, there was usually a faster growth in the economy generally, including consumption. On the other hand, when the military was controlled (in the Eisenhower, Nixon, Bush, and Clinton years), there was great weakness in the overall economy. Eisenhower's policy produced three recessions in eight years, and Nixon experienced two recessions in six years, the last of which was the most serious Great Recession of 1973–75. A great deal of temerity was shown in the Bush administration when it came to serious short-term reductions in the military. Possibly arms can be reduced when we get unemployment falling again, but this great day is pushed into the future.

The Clinton administration had initially been somewhat bolder in reducing the military budget, as mentioned previously. This has already produced relatively greater regional weaknesses in geographical areas, such as Californa, Virginia, and Long Island, where bases are being closed or military contracts not renewed. The victories of the Gingrich Republicans seems destined to increase military appropriations, even for hardware that the Pentagon has no interest in acquiring.

Conventional wisdom holds that the military burden of the Cold War has somehow reduced U.S. competitiveness in world markets. The problem is that a great deal of research and development has taken place as a result of the military and space budgets, part of which has spilled over into the civilian economy. U.S. productivity in manufacturing continues to grow at rates equivalent to or greater than in the past. And there is overall comparatively little depreciation of the dollar in relation to the entire world's currencies in an era of floating exchange rates, including some "dirtiness" emanating from G-5 countries.

There is also a problem posed by the higher-than-average rates of profit being earned in the military-industrial complex. The flip side of the $640 toilet seats is a very high rate of profit in producing these seats. Since a great deal of military spending is still contracted for on a cost-plus basis, this may represent a special problem when profit rates generally are being squeezed by the high real interest rates.

Despite pleadings from Seymour Melman and others that some effort be made to plan conversions of military into nonmilitary activity, the United States—in contrast to Russia, where military spending has fallen by 70 percent—has barely moved on this score. It is assumed that the experience after World War II might be repeated using mostly market forces. As we have seen, however, the situation after World War II was entirely different from conditions today. There is no pent-up demand for nonmilitary products today as there was in 1945. Although fiscal policy was tight in the late 1940s, monetary policy was uncharacteristically easy or neutral.

The conversion of military to nonmilitary production is much more than a question of switching dollars from one account to another. Highly skilled human resources must be retrained for second careers. A post–Cold War GI Bill—including this time the retraining of Sovietologists—would be a logical partial answer to this problem, as it was after World War II.

MERCANTILISM

If the domestic market is weak, can't we rely on foreign markets for disposing of our surplus goods and outlets for investment funds? The problem is that the rest of the world, with a few exceptions in Asia, is probably in worse shape than the United States.[8] As a result of IMF pre-Keynesian advice, per capita growth has virtually ceased in Africa and much of Latin America. The remainder of the advanced capitalist system is more sluggish than the United States, and the former socialist system (except for China) is in shambles. Europe is mired in a stagnation as a result of the ultratight monetary policy pursued by the Bundesbank.[9] For the period 1955 to 1992, the real interest rate in the Federal Republic of Germany has typically been three percentage points higher than that of the United States. The only exception was during the Reagan years when the United States briefly experienced higher real interest rates than West Germany.[10]

Lower real interest rates might again make U.S. investment in the Third World as feasible as it was in the 1970s. But before this is possible, a great deal of the debt overhang must be written off—as recommended by Fidel Castro—and be considered as the foreign aid it in effect was.[11] As the world's economies slow down, it is natural to expect more restrictions on free trade and the development of regional trading blocs, or free trade areas, such as NAFTA. Attempts to restrict imports and subsidize exports are self-defeating. The former will tend to reduce domestic unemployment by creating more less productive jobs, and the latter will tend to produce trade wars.

We should forget about solving our domestic problems at the expense of the rest of the world through "beggar-thy-neighbor" policies. Nor should we expect the United States to subsidize exports through foreign aid or foreign investment that ultimately turns into foreign aid now that the Cold War is over. It is also wrongheaded to expect the United States to train the "talented tenth" from the so-called Third World without insisting that they return to their home countries unless there are political difficulties there.

Our economic problems are solvable using Classical Keynesian monetary and fiscal policy. Monetary policy should be as neutral as possible rather than offsetting an expansionist fiscal policy. We may have to live with some "natural" or healthy demand-pull inflation—due to non-competitive rigidities in the advanced capitalist system—as we approach genuine full employment. If so, we can introduce some form of incomes policy that will deliberately produce higher incomes for workers and lower incomes for nonworkers, in contrast to the Kennedy and Nixon guidelines, which produced the opposite effect.

Orthodox economists argue that stimuli for consumption are all right in the short run, but in the long run we need to hold down consumption in favor of more investment. Classical Keynesianism holds that there is nothing wrong with encouraging consumption, particularly among the lower-income groups, and it may be necessary to taper off the rate of investment (conceivably by government planning) or the "normal" work week as we begin to pay more attention to creating an environmentally friendly or compassionate socioeconomic system.

What Would Keynes Say Today?

Obviously no one can be sure what Keynes would say today, but it seems certain that he would be appalled by many positions of the Bastard Keynesians. We know that he constantly changed his positions on various policies. In fact, he made a virtue of his ability to change his mind when confronted with economic developments that showed that his previous positions had been wrongheaded.

In his *Economic Consequences of the Peace*, he argued that the reparations demanded of Germany by the Versailles Treaty represented too heavy a postwar burden on that country. In fact, the economics of the *General Theory*, as explained by the French Keynesian, Etienne Mantoux, showed that the reparations payments, if spread over many years, would have been employment-creating for Germany. The real problem of reparations was the employment-saving additional absorption of goods and services on the part of the recipients. Thus, when asked by Ernest Penrose, special assistant to the U.S. ambassador to England, to draw up a plan for postwar reparations in 1944, Keynes declared the whole thing a "hopeless muddle."

Keynes changed his mind on the viability of the international gold standard and the so-called quantity theory of money in the early 1920s. Later, in the early 1930s, he recognized that it was investment that determined savings rather than savings being required for investment, as assumed in the *Treatise on Money*.

Keynes was a neo-Malthusian when it came to population, until Hansen's secular stagnation hypothesis convinced him that population growth was a necessary stimulant for the system. His ideas in the

General Theory were rather autarkic and neomercantilist, suggesting that homespun clothing might be preferable to importing cheaper textiles from abroad.

The full employment economy brought about by World War II convinced him that a flourishing international trade brought about by the Bretton Woods Agreement—and pressure on creditors to revalue—held great promise for the postwar years. And his last article in the *Economic Journal* published posthumously in 1946 recognized the virtues of Ricardian trade theory.

By the end of his life, he had become reconciled with von Hayek and contributed a complimentary blurb for the dust jacket of *The Road to Serfdom* in 1946. Robert Skidelsky believes that Keynes would have never approved of military spending to stabilize the system, but it seems more likely that he might have followed his fellow Bloomsbury intellectual, Bertrand Russell, and gone along with the logic of a first-strike on the USSR until the Russians developed their own bomb in 1949. The anti-Communism of his wife, Lydia, would have reinforced his positions. Nevertheless, he also might have followed Russell's later role as a leader in the antinuclear movement.

The economists who most clearly carried out the Classical Keynesian position—in addition to Joan Robinson—were Roy Harrod, Abba Lerner, and Walter Heller. Harrod consistently took an anti–real interest rate position, which was official U.S. policy after World War II. It seems unlikely that Keynes would have gone along with the use of monetary policy as a countercyclical tool as provided for by the Treasury Accord in 1951. Like Milton Friedman, Keynes was skeptical of monetary fine-tuning. Unlike Friedman, Keynes had great faith in stimulative fiscal policy.

It seems likely that Keynes would have treated the crisis in the Phillips curve in the 1970s in some manner similar to Harrod, who in the late 1960s recognized the trade-off between the orthodox demand-pull inflation and the growing inflation coming from the supply side and sluggish growth. The contributions of Abba Lerner to functional finance were recognized while Keynes still lived. Lerner's recognition of "supply-side inflation" would have been welcome in an era when price rises represented attempts to improve the environment and social services generally.

It seems likely that Keynes would have welcomed Walter Heller's distinction between active and passive deficits. On the basis of Heller's tax cut in 1964, Keynes would have seen (like some of Reagan's supply-siders) that the way you achieve greater budget balance is to put resources to work and in the process turn passive deficits into active deficits nearer full employment.

Keynes would have rejected a goal of "zero inflation" because of its deflationary consequences; he realized that the "weighting problem" assures the upward bias of any index purporting to measure the rate of inflation.

As the inventor of macroeconomics, and as the architect of the Bretton Woods framework, Keynes would have certainly been a Global Keynesian, welcoming the final creation of the World Trade Organization. On the other hand, it seems unlikely that he would have gone along with the proposition that the rate of unemployment should be a lever to control inflation, as assumed by contemporary monetarists. Thus, he would have rejected "Penal Keynesianism" brought about by the secular growth of unemployment.

Like Marx, Keynes was a visionary. Unlike Marx, the revolutionary thinker, Keynes preferred evolutionary methods, which would have been reinforced in the nuclear age. He would no doubt have welcomed the ending of the Cold War, but he would have eschewed monetarist methods to effect the transition to a more market-oriented economy.

In short, he would have recognized the general weakness of monetarist theory and rejected Friedman's and Nixon's cavalier conclusion that "we are all Keynesians now."

Development of Keynesianism within the History of Economic Doctrines

Great Britain was the principal source of major contributions to economic thought until after World War II. Adam Smith's *Wealth of Nations* (1776) was perhaps the most famous basis for the classical school, which lasted until after Karl Marx, the great nineteenth-century political economist. But important French economists preceded Smith, particularly the Physiocrats, who considered land as the source of all value, but also the mercantilists, especially Colbert, the great French minister. The mercantilists, whom Keynes admired in the *General Theory*, were found in all trading countries where they had a high regard for gold and silver and for the so-called favorable balance of trade that permitted countries to acquire these forms of commodity money.

The classical economists tended to emphasize labor as the source of value or surplus value. They also tended to look at the economy as a whole for the nation, rather than the economics of its component parts such as the industry or firm. Capital accumulation was considered to be important for growth by both Smith and David Ricardo, who championed the repeal of the British Corn Laws and importation of cheaper foreign grain, thus shifting domestic resources and income away from agriculture into the nascent manufacturing sector.

The early economists began to pursue what seemed at first to be two contradictory goals: the moral philosophical goals of the early Adam Smith, and the later more materialistic thinking found in his *Wealth of Nations*. Subsequently, Milton Friedman would christen these two strands as normative and positive thinking. Still later, Alan Blinder would distinguish between "soft hearts" and "hard heads." The supposed conflict between the goals of equity and efficiency was also popularized by Arthur Okun, Chairman of the Council of Economic Advisers under President Johnson. As Robert Solow has said, most economic discussion involves the distribution of income.

There is an important dialectical relationship between these two broad types of economists, beginning with the optimistic William Godwin and his adversary, the pessimistic Thomas Malthus, another favorite of Keynes. More recently, the argument has surfaced between the optimists, who value the growing role of the state as a stabilizer of economic activity, and the pessimists, who believe that only the unfettered market can solve most economic problems. The latter point of view might also be classified as optimistic, but in my view, it would be false optimism.

Up until World War II, U.S. economists made few lasting contributions to global economic thinking. Henry George's ideas on rent and a "single tax" on land survive in the writings of Harold Hotelling and William Vickrey. Likewise, the approach of the founder of the early twentieth-century institutionalism, Thorstein Veblen, has been continued by John Kenneth Galbraith. U.S. economists also attempted to interpret John Maynard Keynes, who frequently tended to obfuscate what he really meant. The addition of Alvin Hansen's ideas on secular stagnation and Abba Lerner's functional finance represented logical extensions of Keynes's *General Theory*.

Lord Keynes's magnum opus came to dominate mid-twentieth century economic thinking. His main contribution was a rejection of Say's Law—a denial of Malthus's belief in the possibility of a general glut—which had dominated economic thought since Malthus conceded victory to the French economist J.B. Say in the early nineteenth century. He also produced a return to the classical school's emphasis on the economy as a whole, which the neoclassical school of his mentor, Alfred Marshall, downplayed in favor of a partial equilibrium analysis of the firm or the consumer.

Up until Keynes (starting with Marshall) all economics was microeconomics, and the whole was simply the sum of its parts. Keynes's great insight—arising out of the Great Depression—was that what was good for the part might be harmful for the whole. In Keynes's "paradox of thrift," the attempt to save more might actually result in less saving in the aggregate. Thus, saving might be helpful for individuals but harmful for an economy mired in unemployment. It is interesting to note that Keynes, in his own writings, failed to distinguish between neoclassical and classical economics, instead lumping the former into the latter. Thus the distinction between the classical school based on labor as a source of value and the neoclassicals, who recognized the productivity of capital, was blurred.

Although Keynes should receive credit for what is now referred to as macroeconomics—which itself gave rise to Simon Kuznets's national income and product accounting—other world economists and policy-makers were practicing antideflationary policies and saying virtually the same thing as Keynes in other languages: Michael Kalecki in Polish; Bertil Ohlin in Swedish; Hjalmar Schacht in German; and Korekiyo Takahashi in Japanese.[1] The economic prosperity of the United States during World War II seemed to confirm the validity of the *General Theory*. Milton Friedman, who would later father monetarism as the counterrevolution to Keynesian thinking, became disillusioned during the war; Arthur Burns held out for the optimistic belief (correctly, as it turned out) that the postwar period would produce prosperity rather than the depression that most Keynesians feared would appear without the stimulus of increased government spending.

Among the converts to Keynesian thinking at Harvard in the 1930s was the young Paul Samuelson, who admitted that one of the things he would have to answer for at the "pearly gates" would be the increased mathematization of economics. By the 1950s—the decade of McCarthy-ism in the United States—all certified economists were expected to be able to express themselves in mathematical terms. The study of econom-ics would resemble that of physics, so that predicting future economic developments seemed possible. The other side of this coin was the deemphasis on the study of history. Lord Keynes, Gunnar Myrdal, and Joseph Schumpeter all had warned against the substitution of mathe-matics and its preciseness for the study of history.

Another branch of economics after World War II developed around the growth problems of the Third World, for which Keynesian thinking was inadequate. There was an early conflict between the International Monetary Fund (IMF) and the so-called structuralist school, which tended to reject the international division of labor and favor import-substitution by the developing countries. Gradually, the IMF convinced policymakers in the Third World that they should adopt monetarist free-market thinking and rely on export-driven growth policies. Global economic policies based on international specialization and a world-wide market for both direct and portfolio capital would henceforth ensure development in poor countries. In carrying out IMF policy directions—following a currency devaluation—the recipients of foreign investment would be expected to carry out "structural adjustment programs," relying on the market with a minimum of government interference. The original term "structuralist" had been turned on its head.

The economic principles textbook by Paul Samuelson in 1947 repre-sented an attempt to develop a Keynesian neoclassical synthesis. Key-nesian macroeconomic tools would be used by the state to achieve full employment, and thereafter the microeconomic principles of neoclassical Marshallian economics would be applicable. Market reactions and revealed preferences led to all best-selling textbooks at the introductory level being clones of Samuelson's pathbreaking economics textbook. Samuelson rejected the deflationary prescriptions encouraged by the believers in the international gold standard, and in his first edition was willing to concede that inflation rates of as high as 5 percent per year might be required to maintain full employment.

Samuelson also welcomed the Treasury-Fed Accord of March 1951, which ended almost a decade of neutral monetary policy, maintaining that an active monetary policy could be a useful tool in stabilizing the trade-off between inflation and unemployment. By 1957, John Kenneth Galbraith in his *Affluent Society* recognized that 7 percent unemployment might be required to control inflation as a problem, and a New Zealander, A.W. Phillips, would depict graphically the supposed historic trade-off between inflation or increases in money wages and unemployment. The first two postwar decades are sometimes pictured as the "golden age" of the advanced capitalist system. Productivity and gross domestic product in both the advanced and underdeveloped countries were growing at rates that exceeded those for previous periods. By 1960, however, it seemed possible that the rapidly growing Soviet-type economy might actually overtake Western capitalism, as Nikita Khrushchev had predicted. In response, Walter Heller, as chairman of John F. Kennedy's Council of Economic Advisers, carried out a "New Economics" program that produced—as a result of increased military expenditures and cuts in tax rates—a continuation of rapid growth in the U.S. economy.

In the late 1960s, however, there was a sharp decline in the rate of increase in labor productivity in the United States, along with an acceleration of inflation. The combination of growing unemployment and inflation was labeled "stagflation." At the same time, the ideas of Milton Friedman, which were now labeled "monetarism" in 1968 by Karl Brunner, were gaining adherents. One key position was that fixed rates of exchange were responsible for the so-called balance-of-payments problem. The Nixon administration was receptive to the Friedman solution of floating exchange rates, and the Paul Volcker group working in the Treasury Department came up with Nixon's New Economic Policy: a devaluation of the dollar euphemistically known as a "closing of the gold window" and the beginning of the end of fixed rates of exchange supervised by the International Monetary Fund.

The members of the Organization of Petroleum Exporting Countries (OPEC) eventually retaliated for the sudden deterioration of their terms of trade (since oil was priced in U.S. dollars). In November 1973 they administered a huge increase in oil prices, which Charles Schultze recognized to be the equivalent of a large excise tax imposed on the advanced capitalist countries that imported their oil. This increase in oil prices coincided with the Great Recession of 1974–75. It became conventional wisdom that by the mid-1970s the Phillips curve—now represented by the lack of trade-off between inflation and unemployment—was in crisis.

The crisis in post-Keynesian thinking gave a stimulus to monetarism as an alternative to Keynesian demand management and fueled the development of supply-side economics. The pioneer article by Robert Mundell appeared in *The Wall Street Journal* in 1974, and by the late 1970s, the Kemp-Roth bill was floated in Congress, calling for three successive 10 percent annual cuts in the rates of income taxation. What was lacking was a frank admission that the Republican Party was building its program on the basis of the Democratic tax cut of 1964. If the earlier tax cut could almost balance the budget in 1965, it seemed logical that three successive tax cuts in the Reagan years would produce a balanced budget by 1984. The problem was that by the early 1980s real interest rates had skyrocketed to postwar heights and thereby offset some of the potential stimulation coming from increased military spending and the tax cuts.

Although Reaganomics produced an upturn in growth and profit rates—both of which had become sluggish after 1966—the monetarist paradigm began to experience problems in explaining the erratic behavior of the velocity of money rather than its presumed stability. Milton Friedman's ideas began to suffer problems of predicting inflation based on changes in the supply of money. In early 1984, Friedman was predicting double-digit inflation by the end of the year on the basis of the large expansion of monetary aggregates in 1983. Instead, the rate of inflation continued to fall, in part because of William Casey's success in obtaining lower oil prices.

Out of this impasse, a number of deviations from both Samuelsonian post-Keynesian and the monetarist schools of thought blossomed: Rational Expectations, New Classical, and New Keynesian. In addition, the non-Samuelson Post Keynesians (without a hyphen) coming out of the Vietnam War, now led by Paul Davidson, were still gaining young adherents. There was even a revival of the so-called Austrian school based on the writings of Friedrich von Hayek and Ludwig von Mises. What had begun as a search for "Economics as a Science" was now best described as many flowers blooming in the field of economics.

Along with the continuity of the search for scientific economics, there seem to have been changes in the relative strengths of global versus nationalist approaches to economics. Within U.S. economic thinking, this has produced a declining interest in antitrust prosecution and the noncompetitive activities of trade unions. It has been argued that international competition will overcome national monopoly power. By 1995, there seemed to be a developing consensus that global planning for freer trade represented the wave of the future. The final creation of the World Trade Organization in 1994, which had been planned at Bretton Woods fifty years earlier, represented what appeared to be a defeat for national protectionism.

On the other hand, there seems to be a similar secular increase in worldwide unemployment rates, which according to the International Labour Organization are now higher than they have been at any time since the Great Depression. Protectionist sentiment naturally thrives in this environment. Unless the unemployment trends are reversed, the flowering of freer trade seems at best to be problematic in the long run.

There is also a renewed strength to mercantilist thinking, which Adam Smith had hoped to eliminate. Although export surpluses do help individual parts of an economy, for the nation as a whole, the fruits of international trade are still found in its imports, a point well made by Paul Krugman in his critique of industrial policy. In contrast to the policies of the early mercantilists, however, gold has virtually disappeared as a basis for economic institutions. In this respect, Keynes would have approved.

Optimists will tend to minimize the birth pangs of the increased globalization of economics: the internationalization of finance; the rise of international currency speculation producing wildly fluctuating exchange rates; the loss of control over domestic policy by central banks; the decline of national sovereignty; the universal worry over deficit financing; and the high real interest rates administered by the Bundesbank and the Fed. The pessimists, epitomized by Gingrich Republicans, on the other hand, will predict and even work for a return to the national economics of the 1920s that led to the Great Depression. In the meantime, the search for scientific economics continues.[2]

Appendix B

What Is Military Keynesianism (and What Is the Alternative)?

With the ending of the Cold War, one of the great underlying forces responsible for Military Keynesian economic policies has seemingly disappeared. A great deal of uncertainty in the minds of the electorate in 1992 no doubt reflected the realization that some new economic policies were called for. What are the possibilities for future non–Cold War economic policy? Before answering this question, however, we might review the various postwar U.S. administrations with regard to the degree of Military Keynesianism associated with each president.

At the outset, we should realize that all practicing Keynesians have been Bastard Keynesians. Since 1951 and the Treasury Accord, we have been subjected to an active rather than a neutral monetary policy dictated by the independent Federal Reserve Board. Instead of producing the "euthanasia of the rentier," as prescribed by the *General Theory*, it has produced the relative enrichment of the rentier. Real wages and profits have been squeezed by real interest rates, particularly in the Reagan-Bush-Clinton era.

All our Keynesian fiscal policies have been of the "Commercial Keynesian" variety, a label originating with the late Robert Lekachman. Whereas Keynes was comparatively neutral with respect to the two blades of fiscal policy—increasing spending or the cutting of tax rates—practicing postwar Keynesians in the United States have favored tax cuts over nonmilitary spending increases. If federal expenditures were to be expanded, they have usually involved military spending or nonmilitary spending under a military label, such as the National Defense or "Eisenhower" highways.

Whenever we have two variables—such as military spending and Keynesian economic policy—and each variable has its opposite (in this case, nonmilitary spending and non-Keynesian economic policy), we can assume that there are four possible combinations of policies. As it turns out, we have at least one postwar administration representing each of these four possible combinations.

The most common combination comprises the Military Keynesians as represented by Roosevelt during World War II, Truman, Kennedy-Johnson, and Reagan. Although Reagan's advisers never admitted to being Military Keynesians, Murray Weidenbaum, his first chairman of the Council of Economic Advisers, was a pragmatist, claiming that his (Keynesian) countercyclical program—increased military spending and tax cuts—was already in place at the beginning of his recession in 1981.

The next most popular combination comprises the nonmilitary non-Keynesians: Eisenhower, Ford, and probably Bush. The only nonmilitary Keynesian was Nixon; Carter was the only military non-Keynesian.

By "Keynesian," I am referring to the fact that they pursued an "easy" fiscal policy. That is, they were either willing to lower tax rates or unwilling to raise them in an effort to balance the federal budget. Thus, balancing the budget becomes less important than stimulating the economy with budget deficits. The non-Keynesians tended to raise tax rates or refuse to lower tax rates and were overly worried about balancing the federal budget.

By "military," I am referring simply to the use of military spending to stimulate the economy. The nonmilitary presidents—Eisenhower, Nixon and possibly Bush in his last year—either put a lid on military spending or actually reduced military spending or got our Allies to pick up the tab.

While FDR was a military Keynesian during World War II, he was not the world's first Military Keynesian. This honor goes to either Korekiyo Takahashi, the Japanese minister of finance who was assassinated in February 1936 (possibly for reluctance to go further) or to Walther Funk after the resignation of Hjalmar Schacht. They increased military spending in the 1930s to get Germany's and Japan's unemployed resources back to work. At the same time, they neutralized monetary policy by freezing or lowering real interest rates. It was largely in the late 1930s that Hitler increased military spending at full employment, thereby causing Schacht to resign his post as the foremost economic adviser. His replacement, Funk, is given credit for the "New World Order"—the 1940 postwar plan for the reorganization of world trade by a "victorious" Germany—that stimulated the first draft of the Bretton Woods Agreement by Lord Keynes in the early 1940s.

Like Hitler and Takahashi, Roosevelt neutralized monetary policy in early 1942 by freezing or "pegging" the money or nominal interest rate at roughly 2 percent. This limit on money interest continued well after the war in order to facilitate the servicing of the huge postwar national debt as cheaply as possible. By the end of the war, the national debt was equivalent to 130 percent of the gross national product of that time. In recent years, this percentage has been as low as 30 percent of GNP although it is closer to 50 percent at present. Still, it is one of the lowest percentages in the advanced capitalist world.

During the postwar years, there were significant negative real interest rates, averaging minus 8 percent from 1946 to 1948. It was only after the Treasury Accord of March 1951 that the Fed recovered its power to administer higher interest rates. For many years, up to the Carter-Reagan years, the bankers were only able to raise money interest rates at about the same pace as the rate of inflation so that the real interest rates were minimal. In the three decades from 1950 to 1980, the average real interest rate was less than 1 percent.

Military Keynesianism got a big boost from NSC-68 in early 1950 before the outbreak of the Korean conflict. Political scientists ordinarily associate NSC-68 with Paul Nitze, who was more responsible for the military strategy contained therein. Nitze was an undergraduate economics major at Harvard before the Keynesian Revolution and it seems fair to assume that Leon Keyserling, who had been active in economic policymaking during the New Deal, was the principal architect of the economic policy contained in this secret memorandum of the National Security Council that was declassified by Henry Kissinger in 1975.

Leon Keyserling, who by then had replaced Edwin Nourse as acting chairman of the Council of Economic Advisers, argued for a threefold increase in military spending. At the time, the economy was mired in the first postwar recession (despite the stimulus coming from the Marshall Plan and Point 4 program) and unemployment was running at over 7 percent. In Keyserling's thinking, there would be no need for any cuts in consumption to bring this about. In arguing for this paradigm, Keyserling cited the U.S. experience in World War II when military spending grew to as much as 50 percent of the GNP along with significant increases in consumption as evidence of the huge underutilized potential of the U.S. economy to deliver both more guns and more butter.

Sure enough, the level of U.S. military spending more than tripled during the Korean conflict at the same time that consumption continued to rise. Unemployment melted to less than 3 percent, inflation was muted by "price controls," and there was very little increase in the budget deficit, in contrast to World War II. In fact, the first year of the Korean War produced a surplus in the budget, as newly employed resources (labor and capital) began to pay taxes. When Eisenhower eliminated price controls, as promised during his election campaign, prices actually fell a bit, indicating that these wartime price controls were of minimal importance.

The Eisenhower regime represented a serious departure from Military Keynesianism. In addition to putting a lid of roughly $40 billion on the Pentagon annual budget, Eisenhower took a benign neglect approach to the economy during his three recessions. His second recession in 1958 is highly instructive since it produced the largest annual deficit of the postwar years until that time. It is the earliest example we have of a passive deficit emanating from the revenue side of the budget as unemployed resources are not required to pay taxes. About the only thing that Ike was willing to do was to make a special appeal on television to U.S. consumers to go out and buy more automobiles. Likewise, in his third recession in 1960, he refused to stimulate the economy in any way and thus insured the defeat of Richard Nixon by a narrow margin.

John F. Kennedy's "New Economics" represented a strong revival of Military Keynesian policies. In campaigning for office, Kennedy pointed out that his predecessor had presided over a growing "missile gap" and promised that he would rectify this situation. Early in his administration, following his Vienna confrontation with Nikita Khrushchev, he fulfilled his campaign promises, even though the missile gap was nonexistent. As a result, military expenditures, the space program, and foreign aid all grew more rapidly than GNP during JFK's first year. In June of his second year, he made his memorable commencement address at Yale University in which he abjured the need for annually balancing the budget, as had been the practice of previous administrations. He and his economic advisers, headed by Walter Heller, came up with the investment tax credit, or a tax reduction for investors, along with plans for a cut in the personal income tax.

At the time of his assassination in November 1963 the plans for cutting personal income taxes were bottled up in congressional committees. But Lyndon Johnson was able to push the tax cut through a contrite Congress in early 1964, which very nearly balanced the budget in 1965, as previously unemployed resources—labor and capital—began to pay taxes. It was this experience that later influenced the supply-siders (a.k.a. Commercial Keynesians) of the late 1970s and produced a belief by the Reagan administration that the budget would be balanced by 1984 as a result of three successive, substantial tax cuts.

Late in the Johnson administration, on July 1, 1968, fiscal policy became tighter with the imposition of the 10 percent surcharge on the income tax. It was this surcharge that produced the last small surplus in the federal budget of 1969 in the short run, and helped bring about the first Nixon recession beginning in late 1969. Nixon shortly got rid of the tax surcharge as the economy entered the recession—a recession that would bring about a new record in budget deficits amounting to roughly $90 billion during Nixon's first term.

Later, in January 1971, Nixon would announce that he too was a Keynesian as a result of these passive deficits. But he still clung to the notion that he was balancing the budget at full employment as a result of a calculation of the high employment budget balance. If, instead of 7 percent unemployment there was only 4 percent unemployment, the hypothetical or calculated budget would be in balance.

Rather than increase military spending, Nixon actually cut real military spending in each of his six years in office. To get the economy out of his recession, he relied instead on the neomercantilist devaluation of the dollar in August 1971 to stimulate the economy at the expense of certain U.S. trading partners, particularly Japan and Western Europe. As a result of the Nixon shock, by election time the following year, the economy was booming while prices were controlled to some extent by the wage and price guidelines introduced three months after the devaluation.

Gerald Ford's years saw some small increases in military spending, but they were chiefly noted for the tightness of fiscal policy during the Great Recession of 1973–75. In fact, at the September 1974 summit, the administration was still hoping for support in bringing about a tax increase to cool off what was actually supply-side inflation stemming from OPEC's oligopolistic pricing cartel. Fortunately, the House of Representatives, led by Al Ullman, passed a tax cut that the president signed in early 1975. At that time, Ford admitted that he had changed his policy 180 degrees. After this, the economy climbed out of the deep hole created by the procrastination of Ford and his CEA chairman, Alan Greenspan.

Jimmy Carter was more generous with military spending. Campaigning for a second term in 1980, he could justifiably brag that he was the largest peacetime military spender in history. Through NATO, he also pressed our Allies in 1977 to commit themselves to annual 3 percent increases in real military spending until the year 1985. In addition, during his campaign for reelection, he refused to consider tax cuts until he balanced the budget, thereby renouncing the Bastard Keynesian economics of the Kennedy-Johnson years. When he turned over the office of the presidency to Ronald Reagan in January 1981, he also left a four-year plan for increased Pentagon spending, which Reagan barely fulfilled. Carter is the best example we have of a military non-Keynesian, although both Ford and Bush must also be considered for possible inclusion in this group.

President Reagan's supply-side program, which was modeled after the Kemp-Roth bill of the late 1970s, called for three successive tax cuts of about 10 percent, although the first cut amounted to only 5 percent since it took some time (and an attempted assassination) to enact this bold easy fiscal policy. As mentioned previously, on the basis of the experience with the 1964 tax cut, it was assumed using "dynamic scoring" that revenue would flow in to balance the budget by 1984.

The reason why the expected result failed to occur lies in the now increased power of the Federal Reserve Board of Governors headed by Paul Volcker. Volcker at first pretended to be a Friedmanite in late 1979 and stopped worrying about interest rates, concentrating instead on producing a regular growth in the money supply. As a result, money or nominal interest rates skyrocketed and brought about the deep second half of the double-dip recession beginning in 1981 and lasting for a year and a half. At this point, Murray Weidenbaum, chairman of the CEA, announced that his antirecession program was already in place: military spending was booming and taxes were being cut simultaneously. But the strength of the economy was still being eroded by the highest real interest rates of the twentieth century, as inflation collapsed and money rates were "sticky," declining more slowly than prices generally. Thus, the growing slack in the system was producing essentially passive deficits which result from idle labor and capital incapable of paying taxes.

Despite the largest deficits of the twentieth century—which resulted in a tripling of the national debt—Reagan held to his Military Keynesianism and refused to raise income tax rates for the remainder of his term in office. While the rate of growth in military spending slackened in his later years, he still held firm in pushing for Star Wars or the Strategic Defense Initiative (SDI). That he was a Military Keynesian also accounts for the fact that Walter Heller, JFK's chief economist, was nearly brought into the policymaking process of the Reagan administration, much to the consternation of Martin Anderson and fellow economists on the President's Economic Policy Advisory Board. Heller responded by conceding that he was the first practicing supply-side economist under JFK, although he didn't have the genius to label it as such.

The economics of the Bush administration were very different from that of his predecessor, as recognized by Milton Friedman in his Op-Ed piece on "Oodoov Economics" or "Reverse Reaganomics." In fact, when Bush was competing with Reagan for the presidency in 1980, he coined the term "voodoo economics" to describe supply-side economics. His administration was full of retreads from the Ford years, which were clearly non-Keynesian. Alan Greenspan was now in charge of monetary policy although his advice was also sought regarding fiscal policy. As we entered the Gulf War, he sagely advised Bush not to raise taxes and headed a committee to study the possible reduction of capital gains taxes. By inducing our United Nations allies to pay the cost of this war, Bush may have narrowly avoided being labeled a Military non-Keynesian.

The Clinton New Democrats are being advised by the liberals to come up with an economic policy that is not Military Keynesian. In my view, it should be nonmilitary Keynesian, the ostensible economics of Richard Nixon. But this policy should be more aggressive than the weak Keynesian policies of Nixon. Something close to the thrust of JFK's and Reagan's fiscal policy is required. And at the Fed, someone close to William McChesney Martin, chairman of the Fed in the Kennedy-Johnson years, rather than Alan Greenspan, is called for. Better yet, we need another Fed chairman in the mould of Marriner Eccles—perhaps the current deputy chairman, Alan Blinder—who presided over the pegged low interest rates of FDR and Harry Truman in the 1940s.

Although one can appreciate the thrust of both Kennedy's and Reagan's fiscal policies—both of which produced the longest sustained periods of growth since World War II—there is a serious problem with the structure of both fiscal policies and the results therefrom. The results of both policies have been favorable for profits and less favorable for workers' wages.

The Kennedy wage-price guideposts produced an upsurge in the share of profits in total income. Although real wages increased during these years in the early 1960s, they failed to capture a proportionate share of the rapid productivity increases being achieved. During the Reagan upswing, real wages were declining as profits recovered somewhat from the dismal profits picture of the '70s.

Both periods of "Seven Fat Years" were followed by sluggish growth in the Nixon and Bush years and a failure to utilize the capacity created in the years of expansion. Contrary to the economics of Tugan-Baranowsky, it is simply not feasible to constantly subsidize or favor investment without some attention being paid to the consumption power of workers.

The Clinton budget plans for the next five years were comparatively non-Keynesian, in part due to the influence of Ross Perot and Newt Gingrich on our national budget dialogue. Although there is some Keynesian influence coming from Robert Solow, James Tobin, Laura Tyson, and Alan Blinder, the practical politicians are thus far determining overall policy. In the words of Labor Secretary Robert B. Reich, "This is not a political climate in which John Maynard Keynes would flourish."[1]

Appendix C

Thinking about the Partial Devaluation of the Dollar

I have been puzzled by the U.S. devaluation of the dollar in 1971 for over two decades. My original, heretofore unpublished analysis written in the week after the devaluation is reproduced in the following. Subsequently in October 1987 I critically re-evaluated my original analysis; this is also included at the end of this appendix.

Writing in 1995, we now have the advantage of several biographies that have been referred to in the text. The works of James Reston, Jr., and William Neikirk are especially illuminating in this regard.

It now seems clear that Nixon's New Economic Policy had been in the works for some time. The chief architect turns out to have been Paul Volcker, although the actual timing of the devaluation was a political decision. When the Nixon advisers were convened at Camp David on the weekend of August 15, 1971, President Nixon and John Connally, the secretary of the treasury, had already agreed on the so-called Volcker Group's package—both the closing of the gold window and the wage and price freeze. All of the economists present—Paul McCracken, Herbert Stein, and Arthur Burns—argued against the plan, but politics prevailed. The economy was too sluggish in recovering from the Nixon recession, and the reelection was only a little more than a year away.

Both Nixon and Connally have subsequently admitted that the wage and price controls were a big mistake, but they failed to extend this judgment to the devaluation itself. I hope I have presented enough evidence to support the position that the devaluation was unnecessary and in fact counterproductive in that it represented the death knell for the original purpose of the IMF—the supervision of fixed rates of exchange. In the two decades since the devaluation and the imposition of the "dirty float," we have seen a deterioration of the growth in the volume, an increase in the volatility of world trade, and the failure to move toward freer trade. As a result, in 1994 the same Paul Volcker headed a Bretton Woods Commission that came up with a recommendation to return to fixed rates of exchange with larger "bands" than previously.

Even the European Monetary System, which reverted to fixed rates of exchange in 1979, has come apart in 1992—thanks to blunt monetary policy pursued by the Bundesbank in integrating the former GDR with the FRG, threatening the viability of the expanded European Common Market. If there is another Bretton Woods Agreement or return to fixed exchange rates, let us hope that some means can be devised to remove the asymmetry between unilateral devaluations and revaluations, that is, to encourage as many revaluations as there are devaluations. Perhaps some sort of United Nations international tax on countries that persistently maintain undervalued currencies and balance-of-trade surpluses might be devised. In this connection, see the recent clearing proposals of Paul Davidson and Robert Guttmann.

In retrospect, we can see that the devaluation worked in the short run and achieved its political purpose, the reelection of Richard Nixon. But in the long run, it can be blamed for the 1973 decision of the OPEC countries to restore their more favorable terms of trade, since petroleum was now priced in devalued dollars after August 15, 1971. The second round of OPEC price hikes in 1979, connected with the political instability in Iran, became the basis for Paul Volcker and the Bundesbank's decision to bite the inflation bullet. The latter then became the basis for the longest period of high real interest rates in the twentieth century. This, in turn, became responsible for the rapidly increasing passive deficits and national debt that seems to worry people these days and for creating Gingrichian pressure for dismantling the welfare state.

ON NIXONOMICS (written August 21, 1971):

On August 15, 1971, President Nixon dramatically abandoned his "game plan" for maximizing growth and minimizing inflation in favor of a New Economic Policy, which he modestly suggested is the most comprehensive economic program since President Roosevelt's New Deal. In what respects does it represent continuity with what Arthur Okun (the last Democrat to chair the Council of Economic Advisers) has labeled the bipartisan consensus? And what are the prospects that it will work before the 1972 election?

Generally speaking, the Nixon package assumes that there are three equally important domestic economic problems confronting U.S. policymakers: (1) inflation; (2) unemployment; and (3) the balance-of-payments deficit. The goal is one of reducing all three. But it is further assumed that there may be some internal contradiction between solving problems (1) and (2).

In other words, attempts to stimulate the economy and reduce unemployment will automatically generate greater inflationary pressures. In the technical jargon of economists, the Phillips curve—which now diagrams the relationship between unemployment and inflation—is assumed to be negatively sloping. Thus, there is a "trade-off" between unemployment and inflation so that any stimulus to the economy designed to reduce unemployment will automatically aggravate the inflation problem.

Briefly, what are the ingredients and objectives of the Nixon Plan? The ninety-day freeze on wages and prices (excluding interest rates and profit) is designed to reduce inflationary expectations and give the administration time to work out some type of incomes policy, which even Arthur Burns (chairman of the Federal Reserve Board under Nixon) now recognizes to be a necessity. (See Appendix D for details on the proposed incomes policy.) In addition, there is supposed to be a $4.7 billion reduction in current federal spending, primarily through a policy of allowing normal attrition to reduce federal employment. There will also supposedly be a 10 percent cutback in foreign aid. The latter two proposals are designed to reduce aggregate demand and thereby moderate anticipated inflationary pressures, but they will also aggravate unemployment should they represent more than mere political rhetoric.

One can easily be skeptical about both of these proposals on the basis of past experience. The reduction in government expenditures would seem to have something in common with the $6 billion "reduction" in such expenditures promised by President Johnson's Expenditure Control Act of 1968 in connection with the 10 percent income tax surcharge in that year. Looking back at the second half of 1968, one finds little evidence that such cuts were in fact made and much evidence that such rhetoric was used simply to mollify the "powerful" Representative Wilbur Mills.

Likewise, despite the rhetorical annual cuts in foreign aid appropriations, the actual foreign aid shipments have had a curious habit of creeping upward year after year. Thus, although the preceding anti-inflation proposals would superficially seem to contribute to growing unemployment, their bark may well turn out to be worse than their bite.

The more positive proposals dealing with the unemployment problem are the repeal of the 7 percent automobile excise tax and the pushing ahead of the $50 increase in personal income tax exemptions to January 1, 1972. This stimulus to the automobile industry is certainly somewhat bolder than the late President Eisenhower's exhortation to consumers to buy more automobiles to help get the economy out of the 1958 recession. In addition, the new protectionism discussed in the following may well reduce the domestic sales of imported cars and give a much-needed boost to domestic automobile production. The automobile and related industries are certainly an important prop for the entire economy, and this may well turn out to be the most significant component of the Nixon package. "What's good for General Motors" is good for GNP although not necessarily for the quality of life in the United States.

Of lesser importance would seem to be the 10 percent "Jobs Development" credit, a thinly disguised and enlarged version of the Democrat's investment tax credit, which the Republicans scrapped in 1969 under the dubious assumption that the economy they inherited from the Democrats was overheated and no longer required this subsidy for investment. It is assumed that this measure, coupled with the already greatly liberalized depreciation allowances, will stimulate lagging investment resulting from depressed profit rates since the last quarter of 1965. The trouble with these subsidies for the investment sector is the unpleasant fact that existing productive capacity is already grossly underutilized. At last report, industry as a whole was operating at 73 percent of rated capacity.

There is also the likelihood that the depressed profit rates in the latter half of the 1960s—unprecedented for a wartime situation—may in fact be an outgrowth of the investment subsidies that were initiated by the Democrats in 1962. In other words, an artificial acceleration of the investment sector tends also to accelerate the decline in the rate of return to capital, particularly when measured as a percentage of capital invested rather than sales.

On the international front, the Nixon Plan seems to represent a dramatic repudiation of the policies for international monetary cooperation emanating from Bretton Woods. No longer will foreign-held dollars be convertible into gold, although presumably the United States still stands ready to provide a floor of at least $35 per ounce for gold. The 10 percent surcharge on certain imports that are not already subject to quotas or are not tropical products coming from underdeveloped countries represents a dramatic reversal of the freer trade posture maintained by the United States since World War II. However, there are some indications that this may be a temporary ploy designed to be used as leverage to get other "stronger" currencies (such as the Japanese yen and the deutsche mark) to be revalued upward. To the extent that this policy is successful in increasing the competitiveness of the U.S. goods abroad and reducing the effectiveness of foreign competition at home, it would appear to be in conflict with the fight against inflation. Higher-priced imports and greater domestic production of higher cost consumers goods seem hardly designed to reduce the escalation in the cost of living.

The foreign trade components of the Nixon package are assumed to be employment creating. But in order for the U.S. economy to create employment (or export unemployment) through its foreign trade sector, some other country must be ready, willing, and able to import the unemployment emanating from our beggar-thy-neighbor stance. At an earlier stage of the recovery after World War II, it was possible for some of the advanced capitalist economies to act in this fashion, thus serving as a built-in stabilizer for the U.S. economy. But this is not so today, as least in the case of the sluggish Western European economies, which were already running a large import surplus from the United States amounting to $2.4 billion in 1970. After all, it is not too difficult to trace present West German problems back to their earlier revaluations of the deutsche mark.

In the long run, to be sure, the noncapitalist world would be more than willing to run an import surplus (because of its nonmercantilist bias) and thereby act as a built-in stabilizer. But until there is a significant increase in Western buying prices for gold, the Soviets seem intent on sitting on their gold hoards accumulated since 1965.

Although President Nixon has given some indications that he hopes for a revaluation of some of the stronger currencies—which would in effect represent a partial devaluation of the dollar—there would seem to be some sound underlying basis for the belief that the United States, because of its overriding significance as a world trader, is probably the only country in the world that does not enjoy the option of a full devaluation. In other words, there are too many weaker currencies tied to the dollar. Nor is there any fundamental need for a significant devaluation to take place since there is very little evidence indicating that the United States, which has been subject to the least inflation of all capitalist countries, has indeed priced itself out of world markets.[1] To the extent that there is a balance-of-payments deficit, it can be traced primarily to military overcommitments abroad, particularly the now redundant armed forces or "permanent tourists" scattered all over the capitalist world.

There is certainly at least a grain of truth in the assertion that President Nixon has taken the wind out of certain Democratic and other critical sails. He has gone along with Galbraith to the extent that he has frozen wages and prices. He has taken a moderate step toward increasing aggregate demand, at least for automobiles and related industries, and he has promised to reduce government expenditures, thereby receiving the Proxmire seal of approval. Furthermore, he has taken a modest first step away from fixed exchange rates, which should please Milton Friedman, and has gone along with the Samuelsonian notion that the dollar is overvalued.

There is also considerable continuity with the conventional wisdom of most Democrats that the three problems are of more or less equal import, and that there is a trade-off between unemployment and inflation. Like the Democrats, the Nixon administration is steering clear of any attempt to curb the undue influence of the monetary community. There is still too much worrying about inflation and the balance-of-payments problem and too little concern for unemployment. There is a continuation of the belief that investment can be constantly stimulated artificially without eventually paying the price in the form of the underutilization of the capacity created by this investment. And there is very little recognition of the fact that this capacity can only be brought into full use if there is an increase in consumer demand, particularly that resulting from a more egalitarian income distribution.

Thus, the prospects for the Nixon package working before the election (or after) are rather dim. What is required is the bringing of the unemployment problem to the forefront and a minimization of both the inflation and the balance-of-payments problems. Once it is recognized that the Phillips curve is essentially flat over a comparatively long segment, the economy can be safely stimulated without looking back over one's shoulder at either the inflation or the balance-of-payments problems.

In this connection, it should be made clear that there are really two separate types of inflationary situations: one due to inadequate supply (demand-pull or classical inflation), and one due to inadequate demand (cost-push or supply-side inflation). It is the latter type of inflation that predominates at 6 percent unemployment rates such as we have today and that would be reduced (as a result of the spreading of our overhead costs properly, less featherbedding, etc.) if we stimulated demand and moved back toward full employment. To be sure, we would eventually be substituting demand-pull inflation for the cost-push variety at some point, but we would at least have goods and services to show for our inflation rather than the idle capacity we presently have.

Between 4 percent and 6 percent unemployment rates, it is as if demand-pull and cost-push inflation were sitting on their respective ends of a seesaw. When one is up, the other is down. Thus, we can see why the amount of inflation is comparatively constant as we moved from 4 percent to 6 percent unemployment rates—from demand-pull to cost-push inflation—such as we have experienced during the Nixon years.

By the same token, we could predict a similarly constant rate of inflation as we moved back from 6 percent to 4 percent unemployment rates.

If the preceding analysis holds, there would seem to be no contradiction between stimulating employment and generating more inflation, as has been assumed by most orthodox economists convinced of the negatively sloping Phillips curve. However, there is a contradiction between the inflation problem and the conventional foreign trade policy, which tries to stimulate exports and reduce foreign competition, since both of these factors (if successful) would tend to worsen the domestic inflation problem.

In summary, the problem with the Nixon Plan is that it treats one major and two minor problems as if they were of equal importance. Furthermore, it assumes some contradiction between fighting inflation and fighting unemployment when, in reality, the conflict is between fighting inflation and the conventional approach to the balance-of-payments problem. But in its fundamental thrust, the Nixon NEP is consistent with bipartisan consensus, and its proponents—Democrats and Republicans alike—are therefore likely to be disappointed in the long run.

NIXON'S NEW ECONOMIC POLICY IN RETROSPECT (written October 24, 1987)

In retrospect, I underestimated the ability of the United States to impose the partial devaluation of the dollar on Japan and Western Europe. By the time of the Smithsonian Agreement in December 1971, the Japanese resistance to their revaluation of the yen had caved in, and the 10 percent surcharge on our imports could be lifted. This revaluation of the stronger advanced capitalist currencies produced weakness in their economies at the same time that the deliberate worsening of U.S. terms of trade produced greater prosperity in our economy. This is the origin of "Turgeon's Law," which holds that strong currencies produce weak economies and weak currencies produce strong economies in an era when beggar-thy-neighbor policies flourish.

Nor could I have anticipated the great crop failure in the USSR in 1972 and the future dependence of the USSR on U.S. agricultural surpluses. After the partial devaluation, U.S. grain exports skyrocketed, and by 1973 agricultural incomes were for the first time on a par with nonagricultural incomes. Farmers borrowed at what appeared to be very low real interest rates and would later suffer from the Carter grain embargo of the USSR and the very high plateau of high real interest rates in the Reagan years.

By November 1972 it appeared that the Republicans' first attempt to employ the political business cycle had worked. The economy was expanding very rapidly by election time. GNP, labor productivity, and real wages were all a significant plus. Overt inflation was held in check by the price and wage freeze and the subsequent Nixon incomes policy (discussed in another heretofore unpublished paper in Appendix D). In fact, this was the first increase in real wages since 1966, which no doubt converted more than a few blue-collar voters to the Republican Party and contributed to the Nixon landslide.

The main loss was ideological purity. The Republican Party, which had heretofore stood for letting the market handle economic problems, had been forced to increase the role of the state. Nixon himself in early 1971 had proclaimed that he too was a "Keynesian," on the basis of a decision to submit a budget that was only balanced at high or full employment. In fact, the $90 billion increase in the national debt during Nixon's first term in office was the greatest increase since World War II.

The Democrats had given Nixon the power to impose wage and price controls in 1970, never thinking that he would use this power and hoping to embarrass him in the next election for his failure to do something about inflation. In fact, however, the rate of inflation had begun to fall after December 1970, so that this drastic decision to impose wage and price controls was only justified to prevent *expected* inflation coming from the anticipated weakening of the dollar. Traditional thinking (as epitomized in the IMF prescriptions for underdeveloped countries) assumed that devaluations were inflationary and therefore required a certain amount of austerity. Both Friedman (a Nixon supporter) and Galbraith (a Nixon critic) were perplexed by this decision, which seemed so at odds with their expectations of the President. As Herbert Stein notes in his *Presidential Economics* (p. 179), his son, Ben, was correct when he noted on his father's return from Camp David that "ideologically you should fall on your sword but existentially it's great."

Using the framework outlined previously, we can see why devaluations in the advanced capitalist system tend to be inflationary. In short, the demand-pull/cost-push seesaw disappears after the devaluation, and both types of inflation work on the same side of the street. No longer do we have the trade-off between the two types of inflation; rather, they reinforce each other. The demand for U.S. exports shot up at the same time that the prices of imported products and raw materials rose. This was mitigated to some extent by the fact that the currencies of countries producing most raw materials (excluding oil) were tied to the dollar and were devalued in relationship to the strong advanced capitalist currencies, which were revalued upward.

Arthur Burns, who was chairman of the Fed, has been criticized for pursuing too easy a monetary policy in the interest of reelecting the

president. My feeling is that this is an unfair charge since the partial
devaluation was sufficient to accomplish this goal. Rather, the Fed
should always be criticized for paying too much attention to the inflation problem and too little attention to the unemployment problem, a
criticism that still holds true, especially in the Volcker-Greenspan era.
Failure to pursue more aggressively an easier monetary and fiscal
policy produced a serious recession in the middle of a major war. The
recovery from this recession in early 1971 was especially weak and
required a drastic solution—one that had earlier been employed successfully by Canada a decade earlier—the deliberate worsening of a
country's terms of trade in world markets. The comparable move by the
Reagan administration has been the Plaza Hotel agreement of the G-5
countries in September 1985, after which a managed "dirty float" produced a weaker dollar in relationship to the currencies of the four other
countries.

Appendix D

Incomes Policies at Home and Abroad

Historically, market forces have been assumed to determine in large measure our distribution of income. Although government interference in the interests of producers (as opposed to laborers or consumers) has actually been the rule throughout most of our capitalist development, it has been possible to maintain the myth that the resulting inequality in the distribution of income was impersonally determined by competitive markets.

It is of course true that gestures have been made in the twentieth century to redistribute the resulting income through such institutions as the progressive income tax or the growth of the welfare state. However, the gradually increasing equality of income distribution—prematurely dubbed by Nobel prizewinner Simon Kuznets the "Income Revolution" after World War II—was more the result of the unique circumstances of the war itself than it was of our modified capitalist institutions. Thus, during the subsequent twenty-five years, the income distribution has remained remarkably unchanged in the long run: rising shares for nonlabor incomes (profits, rent, interest, and dividends) during periods of economic expansion followed by rising shares for labor during the subsequent contractions.

In an effort to bring inflation and the balance of payments under control, most modern capitalist governments have been forced to abandon their faith in free markets and institute formal nonmarket incomes policies—usually in the form of wage-price guidelines—at various times during the 1950s and '60s. It has been assumed that increases in overall productivity set limits to the real amounts that each of the factors of production can obtain from an ever-growing pie. Thus, any sustained attempt by either labor or capital to obtain a larger percentage of increase in their incomes than that permitted by the increase in productivity will simply be inflationary in its consequences.

At the outset, it should be recognized that there are only three conceivable types of incomes policies: those that decrease the share of the growing pie going to labor (or increase the share for capital); those that just maintain the shares going to each factor; and those that increase the share going to labor (or reduce the share for capital). Let us now examine each of these three broad types of incomes policies with illustrations from contemporary economic history.

(1) *Incomes policies designed to reduce the share of the pie going to labor*: In the noncapitalist systems to date, the rule has been such that increases in money wages should ordinarily be less than the corresponding increases in labor productivity. As a consequence, unit labor costs have generally fallen, and cost-push inflation has been of minimal importance in the operation of the postwar socialist systems.[1] Since labor productivity in the socialist world has typically been increasing by 5 percent to 6 percent yearly, this basic policy has still allowed for substantial annual increases in both real incomes and per capita consumption. In addition, communal consumption generally rises at a faster rate than personal consumption in these systems so that the growth dividend going to socialist labor is more adequate than the official incomes policy would superficially seem to indicate. Nevertheless, such an incomes policy does allow for an even greater increase in the share of income going for investment or other nonconsumption purposes, such as defense.

The only country in the capitalist world to have deliberately set out to reduce the share of increasing incomes going to labor has been France. This policy was particularly explicit during France's fifth Five-Year Plan (1966–1970). In announcing this plan, the French indicative planners frankly stated that their objective was to increase the share of the pie going to saving and investment thereby stimulating the overall French growth rate at the expense of current workers' income. This experiment in capitalist growth strategy came to an untimely end with the French worker uprising of June 1968, after which the government was forced to concede especially large wage increases in order to tranquilize the working class. These wage increases, in turn, were responsible for the subsequent devaluation of the French franc.

(2) *Incomes policies designed to maintain the share of the pie going to both labor and capital*: This has been the more conventional policy pursued by the advanced capitalist countries to date. This type of policy was ostensibly the basis of the Kennedy guidelines introduced in 1962.

According to the version of the "New Frontier" economists, if organized labor would agree to limit its money wage demands to 3.2 percent annually (the supposed postwar increase in labor productivity in the U.S. economy), unit labor costs would remain constant and price stability would be assured. In actual practice, a five-year moving average was introduced so that the annual allowable wage increases could rise and fall depending on what had happened to labor productivity during the latest year.[2]

The problem with the implementation of this policy was that it assumed that something approximating absolute price stability could be attained in the advanced capitalist system—a system characterized by monopolistic competition. As it turned out, the most progressive sectors—those producing increases in labor productivity exceeding 3.2 percent—also turned out to be those subject to monopoly power. As a consequence, these oligopolists tended to substitute nonprice competition rather than reduce their prices as required by the guidelines so that the overall price level tended to creep upward, contrary to the original intent of the guidelines.

As a result, organized labor tended to receive less than its proportionate share of the increasing pie; conversely, nonlabor incomes tended to receive more than their proportionate share. By 1966, when the annual cost-of-living index apparently began to rise by as much as 3 percent, it became obvious to labor leaders that they had been sold a bill of goods and that virtually none of their increased productivity was now being passed along to organized labor. Thus, the guidelines broke down and money wages began to rise by approximately 6 percent annually for the remainder of the decade. The actual distribution of income resulting from the Kennedy guidelines—although superficially "fair" to organized labor—was therefore not too different from that emanating from the noncapitalist or French guidelines.[3]

More realistic and fairer guidelines were drawn up by the Canadian government for 1970 allowing for a 6 percent increase in money wages despite the fact that the anticipated increase in labor productivity was only 3 percent. Thus, unit labor costs were realistically expected to rise by 3 percent with the overall price level also rising by about the same percentage. Theoretically, in real terms both labor and nonlabor incomes would be rising by approximately 3 percent yearly. By the end of the year, however, these guidelines were abandoned since by that time the Canadian price level was already rising by less than 3 percent, and an unemployment rate of early 7 percent was apparently sufficient to prevent any further undue inflationary pressures.

The Nixon "Phase 2" guidelines are thus remarkably similar to those applying to Canada in 1970.[4] Like the Canadian guidelines, it is as-

sumed that productivity will increase yearly by about 3 percent. However, average wages in the United States will be allowed an increase of
only 5½ percent and it is hoped that the increase in unit labor costs and
price level can be held to 2½ percent. Thus, as in the Canadian guidelines, both capital and labor would theoretically share equally in the 3
percent increase in productivity.

However, if the overall Nixon New Economic Policy actually produced the desired effect and succeeded in rescuing the economy from
high-level stagnation, it is likely that the increase in productivity would
exceed 3 percent. According to Paul McCracken, ex-chairman of the
Council of Economic Advisers, a 4 percent increase in labor productivity can be expected in 1972. If this increase is in fact achieved, and the
wage increases can indeed by held down to 5½ percent, unit labor costs
would rise by only 1½ percent. Thus, even if the price level rises by as
little as 1½ percent, it would still permit an increasing share of the pie
to be obtained by capital with a correspondingly smaller share of the
pie going to labor. In this manner, profits, which have been depressed
of late, would presumably be improved as required by Nixon's overall
"trickle-down" strategy.

The difficulties with most of the conventional thinking about productivity are twofold. Nixon, like the New Economists of the Kennedy-
Johnson years, assumes that productivity is almost exclusively a
function of investment in new plant and equipment, that is, of the cost
or supply side of the market. Hence, there is a chronic need for investment subsidies in the form of both accelerated depreciation allowances
and investment tax credits. Despite these subsidies and the substantial
amount of investment that has been forthcoming, labor productivity
has been rising by only about 2 percent annually during the second half
of the 1960s, and capital productivity has actually been declining due
to the growing underutilization of the new capacity resulting from
artificially accelerated investment.[5]

It seems obvious therefore that something more than new investment
producing redundant capacity is required to stimulate the sluggish
gains in labor productivity and resuscitate capital productivity, namely,
more effective demand in the hands and pockets of low- and middle-
income consumers. Were consumer demand to be revitalized, underutilized capacity would come into fuller use, unit overhead costs would
then fall, and both labor and management would have greater incentive
to reduce their present featherbedding practices.

Once it is recognized that more adequate consumer demand can play
a positive role in increasing labor productivity, lowering unit overhead
costs, and increasing aggregate profits, it can be seen that the present
approach by the Nixon administration (and that of the Democratic

"New Economists") to the problem of cost-push inflation is (and has been) basically counterproductive. By attempting to hold down wages (one of the fundamental factors in consumer demand), such a policy simply guarantees the continued underutilization of capacity and reasonable featherbedding, the underlying sources of the high-level stagnation, squeezed profits, the very sluggish recovery to date.[6]

(3) *Incomes policies designed to increase the share of the pie going to labor*: It should be obvious from the preceding analysis that a proper diagnosis of the present problems of the U.S. (and other capitalist) economies requires something more daring than even a maintenance of the existing shares, even if this could conceivably be achieved with the present guidelines. The changes in productivity shown by the two factors of production during the past five years indicate that a larger share of the growing pie must now be diverted to labor, with a smaller share going to capital. Whether this can be effected within the present confines of a capitalist framework is of course problematical. More likely, rather than accept a smaller share of the pie (lower profit rates), capitalists will tend to "go on strike" by not investing, thereby requiring ever-increasing amounts of nonmarket spending to maintain some semblance of full employment.

The only example of the required type of incomes policy actually working today is, surprisingly, to be found in Chile under Allende. One of the first steps of this Marxist-oriented administration was to raise wages by 30 percent and freeze most prices, thus squeezing the profit rates. With more consumer demand, underutilized capacity would be brought back into full production, consumer goods supplies were increased overnight, overhead costs were spread more efficiently, and presumably aggregate profits held up, despite the lowering of the profit per unit. Thus, in the first year of Chile's new administration, real output increased by 8 percent, and prices rose by a substantially smaller percentage than they did the previous year. For the first time, an underdeveloped country has been following a "structuralist" policy rather than that of the "monetarists" of the International Monetary Fund and the World Bank.

The lesson for all capitalist countries (overdeveloped and underdeveloped) is clear. Contemporary inflation is more a problem of a totally unnecessary lack of supplies than it is one of too much demand. By increasing consumer demand, underutilized productive capacity can be brought back into full use and available supplies can be increased in a relatively short period of time. Thus, the remedy for basically cost-push inflation is precisely the *opposite* of that required in the case of the more classical demand-pull variety. As Sir Roy Harrod noted a few years back, there is a natural negative correlation between the two types of inflation so that the correct remedy for one may be a little dose of the other.

Thus, we can see that any attempts by the Nixon administration to restrict wages, reduce government expenditures (including foreign aid), or to hold back badly needed welfare and child-care reforms are in fact poisonous for the present system and can lead only to a perpetuation of the relatively high-level stagnation.[7]

Appendix E

How Keynesian Are the Canadians?

In his *The World After Communism*, Robert Skidelsky makes the following observation: "The era which ended sometime in the 1970s has been called 'The Keynesian Age.' This is a bit of Anglo-Saxon presumption: Keynesian policy was never central except to the managers of the British and American economies, and even in the United States only from the 1960s onward, elsewhere it was added to a portfolio of policies."[1]

If we disregard Skidelsky's overlooking the role of Leon Keyserling in the Truman years, there would seem to be considerable truth in the preceding quotation. This is particularly true in the Canadian postwar experience. According to Robert Campbell, "The Canadian Keynesian approach had certain idiosyncracies which differentiated it from those of other countries, both in intent and with respect to later actions. The Canadian version embraced both the supply and the demand side, although the former tended to predominate."[2]

Like the United States, but unlike Europe and Asia, Canada came out of World War II comparatively unscathed. At the time, Canada had a special relationship with Great Britain, typically running an export surplus with the mother country at the same time that it had an import surplus with the United States. Because of the weakened position of Great Britain resulting from World War II, Canada gave considerable postwar support to the British economy. The Canadian White Paper of April 12, 1945, right after the defeat of Hitler, committed the country to countercyclical fiscal policy and emphasized the positive role of exports. Later, the Canadians pressured the United States to allow European countries to make "off-shore" purchases of Canadian goods under the Marshall Plan. Ultimately roughly 12 percent of U.S. Marshall Plan spending took place in Canada. Since the U.S. economy is roughly ten times as large as Canada's, this represents a more than proportionate share of Marshall Plan largesse.

Although Canadian policy was ostensibly "Keynesian," we might at the outset define what is meant by "Keynesian." Clearly in his later years, particularly at Bretton Woods and in his last 1946 article in the *Economic Journal*, Keynes jettisoned some of his early neomercantilism found in the *General Theory*. His negotiating positions at Bretton Woods on fixed exchange rates, exchange and capital controls, and pressure on countries running export surpluses to revalue, although they were largely vitiated by U.S. negotiators, were more in line with Adam Smith or David Ricardo than with the early Mercantilists. In my view, the Canadian adoption of foreign aid and the assumed need for export surpluses were among the first examples of Bastard Keynesianism, as criticized later by Joan Robinson.

There was nothing in Canada comparable to the Council of Economic Advisers, set up in 1946 by postwar U.S. Keynesians led by Leon Keyserling. Although Keyserling was always careful to classify his thinking as "pragmatist," rather than Keynesian, his policy—particularly at the time of Truman's Executive Order, NSC-68—was clearly Military Keynesian, another aspect of Bastard Keynesianism. According to Robert Skidelsky in his biography of Keynes, Volume II, p. 609, "Keynes would not have regarded armaments expenditures as a rational means of keeping the world booming."

The Canadian counterpart of the CEA, the Economic Council of Canada, wasn't established until the early 1960s, and was actually disbanded in 1991–92.[3] It was created by the Liberals "to assist the government, industry and labour to develop means of encouraging the highest possible levels of employment, of efficient production and of sustained growth for our [Canadian] economy."[4]

Unemployment in both Canada and the United States rose in the late 1940s before the outbreak of the Korean War. The Canadian dollar, which had been fixed at par with the U.S. dollar after the war, was devalued to 91 cents in 1949 following a much larger devaluation of the British pound the same year. This devaluation probably undervalued the Canadian currency relative to the U.S. dollar and reflected the transitional problems connected with reducing dependence on the British market and increasing integration with the U.S. economy.

Canadian participation in the Korean conflict represented the only significant increase in the relative importance of Canadian military spending during the entire postwar era. The U.S. military buildups later associated with the Kennedy-Johnson and Carter-Reagan years were absent in Canada so that we can at least say that Military Keynesianism—a form of demand management—was not a characteristic of post–Korean War Canadian economic policy.

Canada was one of forty-four countries taking part in the creation of the International Monetary Fund at Bretton Woods in 1944. One of its representatives was Louis Rasminsky, who later headed the Bank of Canada, and who was considered part of the Canadian Keynesian group.[5] Both Keynes and Harry Dexter White emphasized the importance of maintaining fixed rates of exchange after the war, with the IMF as the supervisor of these rates, as well as periodic changes, usually devaluations following chronic balance-of-payments problems. In the words of Harry Dexter White:

> The advantage of obtaining stable exchange rates are patent. The maintenance of stable exchange rates means the elimination of exchange risk in international economic and financial transations. The cost of conducting foreign trade is thereby reduced, and capital flows much more easily to the country where it yields the greatest return because both short-term and long-term investment are greatly hampered by the probability of loss from exchange depreciation. As the expectation of continued stability in foreign exhange rates is strengthened there is also more chance of avoiding the disruptive effects of flights of capital and of inflation.[6]

Canada was therefore unique from September 1950 to early 1962 as a result of its decision to "float" the Canadian dollar. The maintenance of a floating currency was certainly something that both Keynes and White would have criticized. Since there was a common belief that the Canadian devaluation the previous year had overshot its mark, it was assumed that the Canadian dollar would float upward and act as a brake on wartime inflation.

Although the Korean War brought growth and prosperity to Canada as well as to the United States, the 1950s generally was not a period of relative prosperity for Canada as it was in Western Europe. During the latter half of the decade, 1955–60, the average growth rate was 2.7 percent, well below par for the advanced capitalist world in its "golden years."[7] The Canadian dollar floated upward until it was worth more than the U.S. dollar by the end of the decade. It was a classic example of "Turgeon's Law," that strong currencies produce weak economies and vice versa in the advanced capitalist countries.[8]

By 1960, the Canadian government began to enter the currency markets as a seller of Canadian dollars, thereby driving down its price. As a result of this intervention, the Canadian dollar fell from around $1.01 in U.S. currency in the first half of 1961 to around 97 cents, and continued to weaken until May 2, 1962, when it was pegged at 92.5 cents in U.S. currency.[9]

It should be recalled that 1961 represented the beginning of the "New Economics" of the Kennedy administration. Walter Heller and his fellow Post Keynesians (Tobin, Samuelson, Solow, et al.) began to stimulate the U.S. economy with a combination of significant increases in military spending and cuts in tax rates. This change from the Eisenhower laissez-faire approach—and three recessions in eight years—produced our first sustained postwar growth for the remainder of the Kennedy-Johnson administration. It represented a combination of Military Keynesianism and Commercial Keynesianism.

This rediscovery of Keynes in the United States can be contrasted with Lester Pearson's critique of Progressive Conservative finance minister Donald Fleming at roughly the same time. Pearson accused Fleming of being a Keynesian, after the Liberals had come to doubt the efficacy of Keynesianism in the late 1950s. According to the future Liberal Prime Minister Lester Pearson: "He [Fleming] is probably the last convert [to Keynes], because if Keynes were still living, he would today, I am sure, reject most of the doctrine put forward in the *General Theory* 27 years ago."[10]

The Canadian devaluation and the subsequent fixed exchange rate were accompanied by grain exports to both the Soviet Union and China, which helped produce the first healthy sustained growth in postwar Canada. In contrast to the United States, Canadian policymakers rejected both the Military Keynesianism and Commercial Keynesianism of Kennedy until 1965, when the U.S. prosperity and a nearly balanced budget coming out of this growth became a model for a Canadian tax cut. Still, Canada, although less involved in the Vietnam War and serving as an important refuge for U.S. draft resisters, probably benefited from the spillover effects of U.S. prosperity in the 1960s.

By the end of the decade, when the U.S. economy experienced the full-blown Nixon recession (1969–70) in the midst of the Vietnam War, the Canadians reverted back to floating their currency in 1970, a full year before Nixon imitated the Canadian devaluation experience in 1962, in an attempt to secure his reelection the following year. When the finance ministers met in Washington in December 1971, where they signed the Smithsonian Agreement briefly patching up a fixed rate system, Treasury Secretary John Connally berated Louis Rasminsky, the governor of the Bank of Canada, for prematurely floating the Canadian dollar.

The Canadians also drew up plans for an incomes policy in 1970, which preceded the Nixon Incomes Policy announced at the end of 1971. According to the Canadian guidelines, wages would be permitted to rise by 6 percent and prices by 3 percent, the difference representing an expected 3 percent increase in labor productivity. The guidelines were abandoned, however, at the end of 1970 (a year before their imposition in the U.S.) since the inflation rate fell to less than 3 percent. Apparently, a 7 percent unemployment rate—in contrast to the prevailing 6 percent in the United States—was considered sufficient to control supply-side inflation, which had already been recognized by Arthur Burns in his Pepperdine College address in 1970.

Canada was less involved in the Cold War than the United States, and was even a late bloomer in the nonmilitary foreign aid field. In 1961, Canadian foreign aid was 0.17 percent of GDP compared to 0.67 percent in the United States.[11] Currently Canada has a program that is roughly three times as important (as a percentage of GDP) as in the United States. Unlike the United States, Canadian foreign aid is rather popular and, in contrast to the United States, the People's Republic of China is a recipient of Canadian largesse.

The OPEC price "shocks" in November 1973 and in 1979 should have been less troublesome for Canada than for the United States since Canada is relatively self-sufficient in oil. Nevertheless, the Canadian price level rose by 10.8 percent in 1975 although the Canadians largely avoided the 1973–75 Great Recession until 1975. Canada did create an Anti-Inflation Board in late 1975, after which the rate of inflation declined to 7.5 percent in 1976 and 7.9 percent in 1977.[12] After 1975, Canadian economic policy became more monetarist, anticipating the Volcker monetarist revolution of 1979–82.

Supply-side economics (a.k.a. Commercial Keynesianism), which came to the United States during the Reagan era, seems to have had little impact in Canada, which at the time was governed by Pierre Trudeau. Although his successor, Brian Mulroney, thought of himself as a Reaganite—and continued the growing nonprogressivity of Canadian taxation—his economic policy and its results were very different.[13] In contrast to the Reagan years, when there was a second long-term expansion resembling the Kennedy-Johnson years, growth fell off after Mulroney took over in 1984. The following table illustrates the different rates of growth in the Trudeau and Mulroney years:

	Trudeau (1968–84)	Mulroney (1985–92)
Real GDP increase	4.1%	2.6%
Employment growth	2.4%	1.7%
Unemployment	7.3%	9.1%
Inflation	7.5%	4.6%
Increase in national debt	+ $180 billion (16 years)	+ $218 billion (8 years)

Source: Pierre Trudeau, *Memoirs*, p. 355.

Canadian monetary policy is heavily influenced by and dependent on the U.S. Federal Reserve. In fact, at a recent conference on U.S.–Canadian trade sponsored by the University of Toronto's Centre for International Studies, George von Furstenberg, visiting professor at the University of Toronto from Indiana University, has argued that "Canada could negotiate a voice in a new North American central bank in exchange for giving up the Canadian dollar and the Bank of Canada," in other words, for being dollarized comparable to Bermuda.[14]

Paul Volcker's success in breaking the back of inflation in 1979–81 also produced a 21 percent nominal interest rate in Canada in 1981. The Mulroney years were characterized by a continuation of monetarist policy (without Commercial Keynesianism or tax cuts as in the United States) under the leadership of John Crow (1987–93), who had previously worked for the International Monetary Fund. It was only by the grace of God that Canada succeeded in leaving the goal of "zero inflation" out of its Constitution, as was the case in New Zealand. This tight monetary policy has virtually eliminated inflation at the cost of double-digit unemployment, a condition that resembles what is taking place in Australia and Argentina.

The Canadian national deficit is very high relative to GDP in comparison with the United States. Part of this is due to the very high real interest rate during the Crow years. By 1990 it was approximately double the rate in the United States.[15] As a result, the average annual growth in the national debt during the Mulroney years was over $25 billion, or the equivalent of $250 billion in the United States (since the Canadian economy is roughly one-tenth the size of the U.S. economy).

Deficit financing is frequently associated with Keynesian economics. But when the growing deficit is the result of passive deficits—emanating mostly from the lack of tax revenue—from high real interest rates, as in both the United States and Canada after 1980, we can assume that this is just another example of Bastard Keynesian thinking. Instead of the euthanasia of the rentiers recommended by Keynes in the *General Theory*, we have been enriching them in the rentier welfare state.

It is important to remember that Maynard Keynes was a Liberal rather than a Labourite or socialist. Keynes had no intention of running permanent budget deficits. "Nor was it Keynes's aim to redistribute income, nationalize the economy, or direct investment or the location of industry," according to his celebrated biographer, Robert Skidelsky.[16] His wartime pamphlet *How to Pay for the War* (1940) was markedly libertarian, in Skidelsky's view. It is also important to note that his wartime plans were less authoritarian than those of the United States and were approved by his earlier nemesis, Friedrich von Hayek.

The fact that Canadian economic policy of the "left of center" has been in the hands of the Liberal Party goes a long way toward explaining the practice of supply-side Keynesianism referred to by Campbell at the beginning of this appendix. Had the New Democratic Party ever come to power outside of individual provinces, we no doubt would have seen more demand management as in the United States.

Glossary

Accelerated depreciation: Tax incentives granted to corporate enterprises enabling them to write off depreciation costs at a rapid rate, thereby reducing reported profits and current taxes. Institutionalized by the Kennedy administration in 1962.

Bank for International Settlements: Perhaps the most conservative organization of world bankers, which supposedly cooperated with Nazi Germany and was scheduled to be dissolved by Resolution 5 of the Bretton Woods Agreement. Originated in 1930 to assist Germany in servicing or paying off its post–World War I loans under the Dawes and Young Plans. The BIS maintains a low profile in Basle, but represents a principal agent of deflationary ideology. Assisted in the bailout of Mexico in late 1994.

Bastard Keynesianism: Term coined by Joan Robinson by 1962 to describe the actual practice of Keynesian policies in the postwar years, including a revival of the belief that "money matters," that military expenditures can be used as a form of demand management, and that exports (loans abroad, foreign aid, or a trade surplus) are an important goal of international trade. Employment creation or inefficiency replaces employment saving or efficiency as an overall goal of macroeconomic policy. The two principal strands of Bastard Keynesianism are Military Keynesianism and Commercial Keynesianism, the use of defense spending and cuts in tax rates to stimulate the economy.

Beggar-thy-neighbor Policies: Attempt by all countries in the 1930s to "export their unemployment." Since export surpluses create jobs, it was only natural for countries to follow neomercantilist policies. The problem was that, since exports and imports are two sides of the same coin, some country or countries must be willing to tolerate an import surplus or trade deficit. In the 1930s, the seller's market or "suction" economies of both Nazi Germany and the USSR fit this bill.

Buyer's Market: Sellers searching for scarce buyers. Characteristic of advanced capitalist-oriented economies in peacetime with problems of inadequate and slowly growing effective demand relative to rapidly growing productive capabilities.

Capital Unemployment: Measured by capacity utilization rates, which are frequently adjusted by the Federal Reserve so as to minimize the recorded unemployment rate. Earlier, McGraw-Hill was responsible for these statistics.

Commercial Keynesianism: Term coined by Robert Lekachman in *The Age of Keynes* to describe policymakers who always prefer to stimulate the economy by cutting tax rates rather than by increasing government spending. Later christened "supply-side economics" in the 1970s by Jude Wannisky, Robert Bartley, Arthur Laffer, Paul Roberts, et al.

Crowding In: Realization of disguised savings hidden by underutilization of productive potential, from income obtained from employment of these previously unemployed resources.

Crowding Out: Assumption that there is a shortage of savings and that government spending diverts savings that might have been utilized by the private sector. Although frequently assumed by supply-siders, there is little statistical evidence for this phenomenon. It's an important component nevertheless of antigovernment ideology. Despite many unsuccessful efforts to demonstrate this phenomenon, it remains part of the neoclassical mystique.

Deficit, Active: Excess of government expenditures over receipts at full employment, however defined. Conducive to demand-pull inflation and the need for an incomes policy to prevent wages from rising faster than labor productivity. Also referred to as "structural" deficit.

Deficit, Passive: Excess of government expenditures over receipts at less than full employment, that is, a deficit coming primarily from the revenue side rather than the spending side of the budget. Popularized by Walter Heller in the 1970s. Associated with supply-side inflation coming from higher unit overhead costs, environmental cleanup, growing sales expenditures, tax increases (including price-raising activities of the OPEC cartel), relative growth of government spending, and high real interest rates.

Deflation: Falling prices accompanied by increasing unemployment and declining growth. Keynes recognized this bias of the gold standard, and recommended at Bretton Woods pressure on creditor nations to reflate. However, he was defeated on this score by the United States advisers, particularly Edward Bernstein. Since then, deflationary policies have been followed assiduously by the IMF, the BIS, and central bankers generally.

Demand Management: Government manipulation of aggregate demand with the goal of producing more or less full employment without significant inflation.

Devaluation: Unilaterally turning the terms of trade against a country. A typical recommendation of the IMF for Third World countries experiencing balance-of-payments problems. For the United States, it involved "closing the gold window" and raising the support price for gold in August 1971. Early in his administration, FDR accepted the theories of George Warren and Frank Pearson, almost doubling the support price for gold—from $20.67 to $35 per ounce. While the universal gold standard was never fully restored after World War I, the thinking behind this nineteenth-century institution remained as a vestige. Thus, flows of gold from Europe were "sterilized" or not counted in the monetary base as an anti-inflationary measure in the late 1930s, supposedly for fear of their inflationary impact.

Disinflation: Generally falling prices accompanied by relatively full employment and rising GDP, as in the 1920s in the United States.

Dollar Gap: The foreign exchange situation prevailing after World War II, when European countries—their economies in shambles—were unable to earn enough foreign exchange by exporting sufficient quantities of goods to the United States, and therefore suffered chronic balance-of-payments difficulties.

Dollar Glut. The situation following the Dollar Gap in the 1960s, when dollars began to accumulate in Western Europe, and the United States began experiencing chronic balance-of-payments difficulties, as in the Kennedy-Johnson years. The positioning of large numbers of "permanent tourists" (soldiers and their dependents) all over the world during the Cold War either underlay or exacerbated this problem.

Dynamic Scoring: Term employed by Reaganite and Gingrich Republican economists to show the long-run effect on the budget deficit of tax reductions.

Effective Demand: Sufficient desire and ability to purchase both investment and consumption goods and services.

Employment-Creating Institutions: Any measure that tends to have as its principal purpose the creation of jobs or disutility, rather than producing utility or satisfaction. Such institutions as redundant advertising, foreign aid, military and space expenditures, welfare programs, unwanted gift-giving, and creative obsolescence might be included.

Employment-Saving Institutions: Any measure that has as its principal purpose the reduction ("saving") of jobs: the elimination of redundant administrative jobs, the introduction of automated equipment, and the welcoming of an import surplus or trade deficit might be included.

Euthanasia of the Rentier: Keynes's prescription for the gradual elimination of real interest as a significant form of income.

"Favorable" Balance of Trade: Mercantilist evaluation of trade balance describing the condition in which the money value of exports exceeds the money value of imports. In mercantilist times, this resulted in an import of gold or specie.

Fiscal Drag: The depressing effect of potential substantial unused cash surpluses in the federal budget in an expanding economy operating at less than full employment. First measured by calculation of the full (or later, high) employment surplus by Walter Heller's Council of Economic Advisers in the early 1960s.

Fiscal Policy: The use of government revenue, expenditures, taxes, and general budget policies to achieve desired economic objectives. Functional finance, under which the Treasury prints bonds for purchase by the Federal Reserve—a so-called monetization of the debt—is a variety of fiscal policy used to defeat Hitler during World War II.

Functional Finance: The theory of Abba Lerner that as long as unemployment exists, the Federal Reserve should be required to absorb new government bonds not purchased by individuals or institutions. There is an implication that tax revenues are only required to restrict consumption. Referred to by conservatives as "turning on the printing press."

General Agreement on Tariffs and Trade (GATT): The United Nations organization created in 1947 and institutionalized in 1948 at the Havana Conference as an alternative to the aborted International Trade Authority planned at Bretton Woods. Its principal objective has been to hold periodic conferences (Kennedy Round, Tokyo Round, Uruguay Round, etc.) to facilitate the reciprocal lowering of trade barriers throughout the capitalist world. The Uruguay Round resulted in the creation of the World Trade Organization (WTO), which should replace GATT. As the most productive economy after World War II, the United States played a leading role in lowering trade barriers through GATT. Later, in 1964, UNCTAD would be organized to represent primarily the interests of the developing countries in the Third World.

Inflation, Demand-pull: Inflation coming from a shift in the aggregate demand curve to the "northeast." Too much money chasing too few goods and services, and the inabililty to produce additional goods in the short run.

Inflation, Supply-side: Inflation coming from a shift in the aggregate supply curve to the "northwest." Higher prices coming from unit overhead costs, including real interest, environmental protection, tax increases (including OPEC increases in 1973 and 1979), and increased advertising expenditures. Produced by lack of effective demand and excess productive capacity.

Military Keynesianism: A variety of Bastard Keynesianism in which increased military spending is associated with an easy fiscal policy, one disregarding the importance of any negative effects of government deficits.

Minirecession: A period of about one year—from mid-1966 to mid-1967—when the U.S. economy failed to grow significantly, despite the rapid escalation of Vietnam War expenditures. A capacity hangover following an investment binge. In the Federal Republic of Germany, this period was characterized by its first actual decline in industrial production. This was the first postwar evidence of the synchronization of economic fluctuations in the advanced capitalist system.

Monetarism: The non-Keynesian ideology first labeled by Karl Brunner in 1968. Emphasizes the importance of changes in the money supply in determining the rate of inflation. Assumes constancy in the velocity of money in the quantity theory of exchange. Also adopted by supply-side economics in the Reagan era in creating a conservative neoclassical synthesis.

Monetary Policy: The management of a nation's money supply so that credit will be available in the quantity and at a price consistent with desired objectives, such as stemming inflation or (less frequently and less successfully) stimulating growth.

Money Illusion: Workers and other recipients of income tending to think only in monetary terms rather than in real or inflation-adjusted terms.

Multiplier: An innovation of Keynesian economics attributed to Richard Kahn and defined as the reciprocal of the marginal propensity to save. A measure of the ultimate effect of increased government spending resulting from a series of respendings by recipients of income.

Neoclassical Synthesis: An attempt by Paul Samuelson in the late 1940s to integrate Keynesian economics into the neoclassical paradigm. If macroeconomic policy were successful in attaining full employment à la Keynes, all of the employment saving principles of classical and neoclassical economics could remain intact.

New Economics: The name given to the fiscal policy pursued during the Kennedy-Johnson administrations, which resulted in eight years of sustained growth, marred only by the minirecession of 1966–67.

Paradox of Thrift: The idea that an increase in saving on the part of individuals may produce a reduction of aggregate saving. Originated in Keynes's *General Theory.* An example of the difference between the parts and the whole.

Permanent Tourists: U.S. military forces (and their dependents) stationed outside the continental limits of the country. Important explanation for the U.S. balance-of-payments problems of the sixties.

Phillips Curve: Diagram of the supposed historical relationship or "trade-off" between changes in the rates of inflation and unemployment. Phillips's original study had wage changes rather than the rate of inflation on the vertical axis. It is assumed that there is some trade-off between these two problems. In the postwar years, there has been a bias toward treating the inflation problem at the expense of the unemployment problem. In the eyes of monetarists (in the IMF and the Fed) it is frequently necessary to "cool off an overheated economy" (i.e., to deliberately create more unemployment to control inflation).

Progressive Tax: A stated tax that takes a higher percentage of income as income increases. This was the goal of the U.S. federal income tax introduced in 1913. In recent years, our tax system resembles a "proportional" tax, due to loopholes favoring higher income groups.

Regressive Tax: A tax that takes a lower percentage of income as income increases. Opposite of progressive tax. Social Security or payroll taxes are good examples.

Secular Stagnation: A long period characterized by the growing inadequacy of investment-like activities to utilize fully the resources released by full-employment voluntary nonconsumption. A hypothesis popularized by Alvin Hansen, the Harvard economist who interpreted Keynes's ideas to U.S. audiences. An assumption that the Great Depression was not simply the result of economic mismanagement—such as the Smoot-Hawley legislation in 1930 or poor monetary policy—but rather the result of endogenous forces operating within the advanced capitalist system.

Seller's Market: Buyers searching for scarce products or labor. A characteristic of noncapitalist-oriented economies, and wartime capitalist-oriented economies with chronic conditions of inadequate supply relative to effective demand.

Structural Deficit See Active Deficit.

Supply-side Economics: See Commercial Keynesianism.

Notes

PREFACE

1. John Makin of the American Enterprise Institute concludes that the inner circle of Japanese economic policymaking is dominated by deeply conservative civil servants who are "pre-Keynesian." They would rather "risk a 1930s style depression" than use deficit finance to stimulate the economy. See Peter Passell, "Japan's Powerful Civil Servants Resist a Dose of Deficit Spending," *The New York Times*, July 22, 1993, p. D-2. Japanese policymakers seem to have been influenced by Paul Samuelson, who typically has argued for an easy money, tight fiscal policy.

2. See the following volumes: Herbert Rosenbaum, editor, *Franklin D. Roosevelt: The Man and the Myth, the Era, 1932–1945* (Greenwood, 1982); William Levantrosser, editor, *Harry S. Truman: The Man From Independence* (Greenwood, 1986); Joan Krieg, editor, *Dwight D. Eisenhower, Soldier, President and Statesman* (Greenwood, 1988); Bernard J. Firestone, editor, *The Quest for Nuclear Stability: John F. Kennedy* (Greenwood, 1982); Joan Krieg, editor, *John F. Kennedy, The Promise Revisited* (Greenwood, 1988); Bernard J. Firestone, editor, *Lyndon Baines Johnson and the Uses of Power* (Greenwood, 1988); William Levantrosser, editor, *Richard M. Nixon, Politician, President and Administrator* (Greenwood, 1991); William Levantrosser, editor, *Cold War Patriot and Statesman: Richard M. Nixon* (Greenwood, 1993); Bernard J. Firestone, editor, *Gerald R. Ford and the Politics of Post-Watergate* (Greenwood, 1993); Herbert Rosenbaum, editor, *Jimmy Carter: Foreign Policy and Post-Presidential Years* (Greenwood, 1994); Herbert Rosenbaum, editor, *The Presidency and Domestic Policy of Jimmy Carter* (Greenwood, 1994).

INTRODUCTION

1. For Robinson's first use of the term in print, see her review of Harry Johnson's book, *Money, Trade and Economic Growth*, in the *Economic Journal*, September 1962, 691.

2. Michal Kalecki, *Selected Essays in the Dynamics of the Capitalist Economy, 1933–70*, Cambridge, UK: Cambridge University Press, 1971.

3. G. C. Harcourt's contribution, *New Palgrave*, Vol. I, 203–4.

4. According to Robert M. Campbell, "The Canadian Keynesian approach had certain idiosyncracies which differentiated it from those of other countries, both in intent and with respect to later actions. The Canadian version embraced both the supply and the demand sides, although the former tended to predominate." See Robert M. Campbell, *Grand Illusions: The Politics of the Keynesian Experience in Canada, 1945–1975* (Peterborough, Ont: Broadview Press, 1987, p. 38). This is reflected in the practice of floating the Canadian dollar both in the 1950s and later in 1970 (before Nixon's NEP and without his permission). Louis Rasminsky, the Canadian top banker at the Smithsonian in December 1971, was castigated by Treasury Secretary John Connally because of Canada's premature action. There was no significant increase in Canadian military spending in either the Kennedy-Johnson or Reagan years.

5. For a synopsis of the position of Keynesianism within the development of economic doctrines, see Appendix A.

6. See my "Conversion of the US Economy After World War II," *Economic Reform*, February 1994, 5.

7. *Business Week*, 23 August 1993, 52–53. According to Soros, the currency crisis was "very reminiscent of what happened during the interwar period between WW I and WW II, and it's really amazing how people haven't learned from past experience. It's as if Keynes had never lived. Some of the same mistakes: overvalued currencies, sticking to monetary discipline in a time of recession, you know, very high real interest rates. It's a tragic situation." See Timothy A. Canova, "The Transformation of U.S. Banking and Finance: From Regulated Competition to Free-Market Receivership," *Brooklyn Law Review*, Winter 1995, 1327.

8. See my "The Forgotten Lessons," *Newsday*, 13 March 1994, 42.

9. See Brian Motley, "Inflation and Growth," FRBSF *Weekly Letter*, 31 December, 1993.

10. See my "Is God a Keynesian?" *Economic Reform*, May 1994, 4. Also, "Brief Economic Boom Seen From Quake in California," *The Wall Street Journal*, 31 March 1994, A-6. Laura Tyson, chairman of Clinton's CEA, and later head of the National Economic Council, has aptly referred to such stimuli as "the flood factor."

11. For an interesting account of the Reagan administration's role in accelerating the fall of oil prices with the objective of defeating the Russians, see Peter Schweizer, *Victory* (New York: Atlantic Monthly Press, 1994). See also Steven Solomon, *The Confidence Game*, where he refers to a "top secret interagency task force" in early 1982 headed by Tim McNamar and including Paul Volcker.

12. In this connection, see Robert Guttmann, *How Credit-Money Shapes the Economy*.

CHAPTER 1

1. Orthodox economists will maintain that the first German "miracle" was simply the result of increased military spending. In fact, however, there was

comparatively little increase in German military spending until after 1936. Public works such as the autobahns were financed by deficits, and women were encouraged to drop out of the labor force and reproduce. According to Robert Skidelsky (*John Maynard Keynes*, Vol. II, p. 48), "by October, 1934, three million workers had been reemployed in Germany over two years, half the previous total of unemployment, and Keynes's silence on Hitler's New Deal was deafening."

2. Robinson recognized Hitler as the first practicing Keynesian in her 1971 Richard T. Ely lecture in New Orleans. The Japanese may have been practicing Keynesian economics even earlier, beginning in 1931. The financial advisers, Hjalmar Schacht (German finance minister) and Korekiyo Takahashi (Japan's finance minister at the age of eighty-one), were both apparently opposed to Military Keynesianism. Schacht refused to go along with increased military spending at full employment and resigned in 1938, thereby saving his neck after the Nuremberg trials. His successor, Walther Funk, former economic journalist, received a twenty-year sentence, although he was released early because of ailing health. Takahashi was assassinated in a military action in February 1936. For an interpretation of Takahashi's policies as Keynesian, see Takafusa Nakamura, *Economic Growth in Prewar Japan* (Yale University Press, 1982). It would seem to be no accident that the German and Japanese editions of the *General Theory* appeared in 1936, whereas the French edition was delayed until 1942. Robert Skidelsky (*John Maynard Keynes*, Vol. II, p. 488) recognizes that Keynesian methods of fighting depression were tried in both Japan and Sweden. Takahashi was unlikely to have been inspired by Keynes, but Lindahl, Myrdal, and Ohlin were in touch with Keynes. John Kenneth Galbraith claims that "in a just world, reference would be not to the Keynesian but to the Swedish revolution" (See his *A Journey Through Economic Time*, New York: Houghton Mifflin, 1994, p. 113). Oswald Mosley, leader of the British Union of Fascists, was also thinking along similar lines in the early 1930s when he was part of the MacDonald government. (See Skidelsky, *John Maynard Keynes*, pp. 395–96. For a discussion of "Military Keynesianism" see Appendix B).

3. "Thus the remedy for a boom is not a higher rate of interest, but a lower rate of interest" (John Maynard Keynes, *General Theory*, p. 322). Like Milton Friedman, Keynes was opposed to countercyclical monetary policy, which helps explain his later inability to understand initially Abba Lerner's "functional finance." This is not always understood by noneconomists. For example, Nathan Miller writes: "Marriner S. Eccles held views that paralleled those of Keynes—without having heard of the English economist—and believed that prosperity could be achieved and maintained by adjusting the supply of money to fluctuations in the business cycle." See Nathan Miller, *F.D.R.: An Intimate History* (New York: New American Library, 1983). Eccles was of course advised by the late Lauchlin Currie, one of the earliest U.S. Keynesians, who was born in Canada and later relocated to Colombia, where he died in 1994.

4. See Roy Harrod, *Towards a Dynamic Economics* (London: Macmillan & Co., 1948, p. 159).

5. As a result of Britain's devaluation, the Great Depression had a lesser effect on the British economy during the 1930s, in contrast to the 1920s, when Great Britain was suffering from double-digit unemployment due to the overvalued pound sterling. It was this decade of double-digit unemployment in the '20s—when other countries were

prospering—that convinced Keynes that there was no full employment equilibrium. See Robert Skidelsky, *John Maynard Keynes*, Vol. II, p. 130. It also helps explain why Keynes paid little attention to the causes of the Great Depression beginning in 1929.

6. Kornai has apparently given up on this term (suction economy), which never caught on among orthodox Sovietologists. See Janos Kornai, *The Socialist System* (Princeton University Press, 1992, p. 22). By the late 1930s, economists joked that the only available German exports were cuckoo clocks.

7. Frances Stewart, "Back to Keynesianism: Reforming the IMF," *World Policy Journal* (Summer 1987): 470. Actually, the U.S. delegation refused to go along with many of Keynes's advanced positions that would eliminate the international currency speculation that has been disruptive in the years since 1971. The virtual demise of the European Monetary System in 1992 and the Mexican peso crisis come to mind in this connection. Keynes's initial draft of what became the Bretton Woods Agreement was a reaction to Walther Funk's "new world order" announced on July 26, 1940, to prepare the world for the results of a German victory over Britain. Funk wanted to demonetize gold, since three-fourths of the world's supply was concentrated in the United States at that time. Keynes also welcomed the elimination of gold, a vestige of the gold standard, which he deplored.

8. Keynes's "statement in March 1932 that saving was no longer the dog but the tail" is a recognition of the passive nature of saving. See Peter Clarke, *The Keynesian Revolution in the Making 1924–1936* (Oxford: Clarendon Press, 1988).

9. Secular stagnation was supposedly based on a completion of the U.S. territorial expansion, relative lack of population growth (including restrictive immigration after 1920), excess capacity, and a bias toward capital-saving technology. Paul Samuelson, in the postwar euphoria over rapid growth, obliterated this concept by later describing the advanced capitalist system as subject to "secular exhilaration." As a result of his acceptance of the secular stagnation thesis, Keynes abandoned his earlier neo-Malthusianism. See Robert Skidelsky, *John Maynard Keynes*, Vol. II, p. 632.

10. This book, according to Robert Skidelsky, is surprisingly libertarian and was approved by von Hayek. See Robert Skidelsky, *The Road from Serfdom* (New York: Viking-Penguin, 1996).

11. The original Volkswagen Works in Wolfsberg survived World War II and continued production in the British zone. Responsibility for its operations was divided between the governments of Lower Saxony and the Federal Republic of Germany. Its success with the "beetle" in the 1950s became an embarrassment to the West German government, committed as it was to the "social market" economy. This ultimately resulted in the sale of stock (a limit of five shares per family) to lower and middle-income workers in the plant in 1960. In the 1966–67 recession, Volkswagen went over to a four-day work week whereas both Ford and Opel fired workers. More recently in 1993, Volkswagen has been experimenting with a four-day work week in a "soft" German economy. The Austrian steel plant remained as part of the state sector after World War II, partly because of Soviet influence as an occupying power.

CHAPTER 2

1. Townsend Hoopes and Douglas Brinkley, *Driven Patriot* (New York: Knopf, 1992, pp. 167–68).

2. Capital unemployment also disappeared. The steel industry was operating at 120 percent of full capacity as a reflection of the downward bias of prewar estimates of capacity and the postponement of capital repairs.

3. The Bank Deutscher Laender (the forerunner of the Bundesbank) was already by 1950 pushing through a high interest rate policy of 6 percent despite 11 percent unemployment. At the time, U.S. interest rates were still pegged at 2 percent. See David Marsh, *The Most Powerful Bank* (New York: Times Books, 1993).

4. See Leon Martel, *Lend-Lease, Loans, and the Coming of the Cold War* (Boulder, CO: Westview Press, 1979).

5. In early 1995, the Germans—as a result of reunification of the two Germanys—agreed to repay interest on bonds earning 3 percent interest. See Floyd Norris, "Hitler Defaulted, but Now Germany Will Pay Debts," *The New York Times*, 6 January 1995, p. D-1. Earlier the Bank for International Settlements announced in its 1980 annual report that the principal of these debts had been taken over by the Federal Republic of Germany and was finally extinguished on June 1, 1980, with the interest postponed until after reunification. See D. E. Moggridge, *Maynard Keynes: An Economist's Biography* (London: Routledge, 1992, p. 542).

6. Peter Temin, *Lessons from the Great Depression* (Cambridge, MA: The MIT Press, 1989, p. 23). Temin concludes that deflationary-biased international monetary policy coming from the international banking community led to the Great Depression. An earlier work, *Did Monetary Forces Cause the Great Depression?*, challenged the Friedman position that the policies of the U.S. Federal Reserve System were responsible, along with the Smoot-Hawley tariff, for the Great Depression.

7. According to Dulles, "to reverse what then occurred and require the Allies to pour back upon us an equivalent stream of commodities ($15 billion) will be more destructive to our laboring and industrial tranquility than war itself." See John Foster Dulles, "The Reparations Problem," *Economic Journal* (June 1921): 186. Keynes was the editor of the journal at the time.

8. For a statement of Harry Dexter White on the importance of stable exchange rates, see Judy Shelton, *Money Meltdown* (New York: The Free Press, 1994).

9. An "austerity program" included a cutback in government investment projects, denationalization of government enterprise, a reduction in food and transportation subsidies, and an attempt to balance the budget—all supposedly leading to stable prices. Adoption of such deflationary policies has frequently produced political unrest resulting in loss of life. In conversations with the late Sol Adler, a close friend of Harry Dexter White, in Beijing in September 1992, I learned that White and Keynes independently came to the conclusion that something must be done to reduce the power of international bankers in the postwar years. The imposition of fixed exchange rates by the IMF presumably reduced the power of the banking community (and opportunities for speculative windfall profits) until after the imposition of the Nixon "shock" by the United States.

10. A mature creditor was the last of four stages, one that characterized Great Britain before World War II. The country in this enviable position would live on the proceeds from its earlier foreign investment and chronically run a trade deficit or import surplus.

11. Why should an oligopoly deliberately forgo short-term profits? At the time, the conventional wisdom had it that they feared possible antitrust prosecution if profits were exhorbitant.

12. Keyserling had a law degree from Harvard but had never completed his Ph.D. dissertation in economics at Columbia University. As a result, he never became a member of the club. Nevertheless, he did eventually become chairman of the CEA despite protests on the part of some orthodox economists.

13. In Canada, the development assistance program inaugurated under the Colombo Plan in 1950 spawned a new bureau administered by the Department of Trade and Commerce in 1951. By 1958, its growth resulted in a promotion to a "branch," and in 1960 it became the External Aid Office, a semiautonomous agency. Its name was changed in 1968 to the Canadian International Development Agency (CIDA). See Kim Richard Nossal, *The Politics of Canadian Foreign Policy* (Scarborough, Ont.: Prentice-Hall, 1985). Relatively speaking, the Canadian aid program is about three times as important as its U.S. counterpart in the early 1990s. Total official development assistance (ODA) was over $3 billion in 1990–91 or 0.45 percent of the Canadian GNP (Canadian International Development Agency, *Annual Report, 1990–1991*, pp. S5 and S60). The Agency claims support by 75 percent of the Canadian population, considerably higher than in the United States, even before the Gingrich Republicans.

14. See *The New York Times*, 30 January 1974, p. 10. Ambassador Moynihan defended the Nixon plan to relinquish $2.3 billion in rupees to India, which was described by Lester Wolff (D., N.Y.) as "one of the great give-aways."

15. In February 1975, for undisclosed reasons, Secretary of State Henry A. Kissinger declassified NSC-68. One of the principal opponents of NSC-68 was Louis Johnson, the secretary of defense replacing Jim Forrestal. Johnson questioned whether the U.S. economy could tolerate significant increases in military spending and the resulting "inflationary" deficits. Thus, the architects of NSC-68 waited until Johnson was out of the country at a NATO meeting in The Hague before pushing through the authorizations made possible by the Korean War. For details, see *Foreign Relations of the United States, 1950*, Vol. I, (Washington, D. C.: U.S. Government Printing Office, 1977). See also John Prados, *Keeper of the Keys* (New York: William Morrow & Co., 1991). In Ernest R. May's *American Cold War Strategy: Interpreting NSC-68* (New York: St. Martin's, 1993), Paul Nitze credits Keyserling with developing the economics of NSC-68. Initially, Keyserling was advocating the use of nondefense expenditures to get the United States economy out of the Truman recession.

16. At the Hofstra Truman Conference in April 1983, I asked Keyserling whether he was a Keynesian or a post-Keynesian. He assured me that he was neither, but rather a "pragmatist." I asked whether he was responsible for NSC-68, and he replied that "it was the lifetime achievement of which I am most proud."

17. See Leon Keyserling, *The Toll of Rising Interest Rates* (Washington, D.C.: Conference on Economic Progress, 1964).

CHAPTER 3

1. The equation of the Quantity Theory of Money is $MV = PT$, where M represents the money supply and V its velocity or turnover. P is the price level and T is the trade or total product. With V and T relatively stable in the short run, the price level is assumed to be determined by changes in the money supply. Keynes's *Tract on*

Monetary Reform in 1923 had already begun to question the stability of the velocity of money. See Robert Skidelsky, *John Maynard Keynes*, Vol. II, pp. 136–137.

CHAPTER 4

1. At one point, President Kennedy decided to raise taxes by $3 billion after the East Germans built their wall. It required a visit by Paul Samuelson to Hyannis Port to dissuade the president from this folly. See Walter W. Heller, *New Dimensions of Political Economy* (Cambridge, MA: Harvard University Press, 1966, p. 32).

2. As the Council of Economic Advisers acknowledged in 1964, "the expenditure increases of 1961–1962, undertaken to bolster defense and space programs and to provide for unmet civilian needs, were highly stimulative to the economy." See *Economic Report of the President, 1964*, p. 46.

3. For a detailed description of the difference between a "free lunch" and a "no free lunch" economy, see my *State and Discrimination*, p. 12.

4. See my "The Enigma of Soviet Defense Expenditures," *The Journal of Conflict Resolution* (June 1964).

5. The problem of distinguishing between active and passive deficits then becomes one of deciding on what level of unemployment is to be considered "full" employment. According to Humphrey-Hawkins legislation in 1978, it was defined as 4 percent unemployment, and the CEA was supposed to make annual calculations as to when this would take place. Calculations did appear in the annual reports of the CEA for several years, but eventually they disappeared. By 1995, *The Wall Street Journal* was advocating the repeal of Humphrey-Hawkins, and the required biannual appearances of Chairman Greenspan before the House banking committee.

6. *The New York Times*, 7 June 1964, p. 42.

7. For a good account of Heller's amnesia and eventual conversion to supply-side economics, see Robert L. Bartley, *The Seven Fat Years* (New York: The Free Press, 1992, pp. 72–74).

8. Eliot Janeway, *The Economics of Crisis: War, Politics and the Dollar* (New York: Weybright & Talley, 1968).

CHAPTER 5

1. Had the training programs not existed, the unemployment rate would have been more like 4.8 percent, rather than the 3.6 percent reported, according to calculations of Professor Robert Horn of James Madison University.

2. Arthur E. Burns, *Reflections of an Economic Policy Maker* (Washington, D.C.: American Enterprise Institute, 1978, pp. 108, 112).

3. Classical Keynesians would consider deficits at full employment as an acceptable goal. See interview with Nobel laureate James Tobin in *Challenge* (May-June, 1992): 16.

4. See *Economic Report of the President, 1971*.

5. Herbert Stein, *Presidential Economics* (New York: Simon & Schuster, 1985, p. 35). At the Nixon Presidential Library in Yorba Linda, California, the Keynesian

interpretation of Nixon's policy seems to have been abandoned, and his wage and price controls following the devaluation are now considered to have been a mistake. Nixon did not concede the 1972 election to George McGovern, needless to say. John Connally, secretary of the treasury, has also admitted that the wage and price controls were a mistake. See "A Conversation With John Connally of Texas" (Washington, D. C.: American Enterprise Institute, 1978, p. 12). Nixon and Connally apparently agreed that if forced to close the gold window, they would at the same time impose wage and price controls. See Herbert Stein, *Presidential Economics*, pp. 166–67, and James Reston, Jr., *The Lone Star: The Life of John Connally* (New York: Harper & Row, 1989, p. 405). The source of Nixon's statement on Keynes is now attributed to William Safire. In an interview shortly before his death, Nixon gave Safire a mock-suspicious look: "Weren't you the one who put me up to saying 'we are all Keynesians now'?" *The New York Times, Op. Ed.* 5 December 1993, p. A-17.

6. Comparisons of the so-called weakness of the dollar usually include only advanced countries, such as members of the OECD, but they often exclude Canada and Mexico, both members of OECD and our largest trading partners, which have weak curencies relative to the dollar. When comparisons are made with all currencies of the world, this weakness evaporates, even for the 1970s, when the dollar showed weakness as currency speculators drove down its price. In the 1980s, the dollar strengthened in the first half of the decade and weakened in the second half owing to the managed depreciation coming out of the Plaza Hotel agreement, so that overall there was little change in the 1980s.

7. George Perry of the Brookings Institution was one of the few economists even to ask whether there might be a horizontal Phillips curve.

8. Early in the Nixon administration, Milton Friedman sent a secret message to Nixon urging him to abandon fixed rates of exchange. See Leo Melamed, ed., *The Merits of Flexible Exchange Rates: An Anthology* (Fairfax, VA: George Mason University Press, 1988). Arthur Burns was sent on a secret mission to Western Europe "to test European opinion on the issue of raising the price of gold" (devaluing the dollar). Later, Volcker, as undersecretary of the treasury for monetary affairs and head of the so-called Volcker Group, worked on the plan for Nixon's New Economic Policy that was eventually adopted on August 15, 1971, despite the opposition of all of the economists present at Camp David. For a good discussion of the preceding development of Nixon's NEP see William Neikirk, *Volcker, Portrait of the Money Man* (New York: Congdon & Weed, 1981), especially "Ninja and the Death of Bretton Woods" (pp. 141–160). Martin Walker, *The Cold War: A History* (New York: Henry Holt, p. 223), claims that Arthur Burns was the one dissenting voice at Camp David. I too once held this belief and personally confronted Paul McCracken with this hypothesis. McCracken assured me that Burns was also opposed to closing the gold window.

9. For a more critical evaluation of Burns's performance, see Alfred Malabre, Jr., *Lost Prophets* (Cambridge, MA: Harvard Business School Press, 1994, pp. 61–65).

CHAPTER 6

1. President Ford had initially wanted a cutback of $17 billion in government spending, which was completely ignored by Congress.

2. Charles Schultze, *Higher Oil Prices and the World Economy: The Adjustment Problem* (Washington, D.C.: Brookings Institution, 1975, p. 65).

3. Pierre Elliott Trudeau, *Memoirs* (Toronto: McClelland & Stewart, 1993, p. 196). From a rate of nearly 11 percent in 1975, the Canadian rate of inflation declined to 7.5 percent in 1976 and 7.9 percent in 1977.

4. This profitability has grown over the years. "Trading is the most profitable business that banks have. Indeed, the six top American banks split profits of more than $900 million for three months of trading activity, which represented more than 40 percent of their total profits." See Saul Hansell, "Europe's Turmoil Aids U.S. Banks," *The New York Times*, 4 August 1993, p. D-1.

CHAPTER 7

1. Woodrow Wilson's first appointment to the newly authorized Federal Reserve Board in 1913 was Thomas D. Jones of Chicago, a conservative industrialist. See August Heckscher, *Woodrow Wilson* (New York: Charles Scribner's Sons, 1991, p. 332). This appointment was criticized by the banking community and by the populists of that era.

2. Carter's Four-Year Plan called for a 5 percent real annual increase in military spending and included allowances for expected inflation of between 9 percent and 7 percent. Since the actual inflation rate fell faster than assumed by Carter, Reagan's actual budget spending in nominal terms was less than the Carter goal. For 1984, Carter proposed $258 billion whereas Reagan's appropriation was $249.8 billion.

3. As Martin Walker concludes, "The dramatic rearmament of the Reagan years was largely envisaged by the Carter Administration." See Martin Walker, *The Cold War: A History*, p. 250.

4. For a good account of the development of supply-side thinking beginning with a 1974 *Wall Street Journal* article by Robert Mundell, see Robert L. Bartley, *Seven Fat Years*.

5. For a fuller explanation of Blinder's Keynesian or nonmonetarist views, see Alan B. Blinder, *Hard Heads, Soft Hearts* (New York: Addison-Wesley, 1987).

6. Martin Anderson, *Revolution*, p. 269. The decision of Donald Regan to eliminate the PEPAB (President's Economic Policy Advisory Board) was shortly reversed as a result of the objections of Milton Friedman and Martin Anderson, so the committee to which Heller was invited to join was never convened.

CHAPTER 8

1. In the words of Martin Walker, "Reagan's rearmament program was a classic example of Keynesian deficit-spending, public investment to lift the economy out of a recession. It certainly achieved that result, and the Reagan economic boom of the mid- and later 1980s was a triumphant endorsement of Keynes's economic theories." See Martin Walker, *Cold War*, p. 266.

2. The Mexican debt crisis of August 1982 eventually forced Paul Volcker to let up on his monetary brakes on the economy and abandon his ostensibly Friedmanian position of ignoring interest rates.

3. According to Robert Horn, "It is clear that the age-adjusted rates under the Reagan Administration have been consistently higher than those experienced during the Carter Administration." See *Challenge* (July-August 1988): 57.

4. Leonard Silk,"The Crucial Issues Politicians Ignore," *The New York Times*, 24 April 1992, p. D-2.

5. Until this announcement, the G-5 countries had held secret meetings, and this pronouncement apparently put an end to these smaller group meetings. See Paul Volcker and Toyoo Gyohten, *Changing Fortunes* (New York: Times Books, 1992, p. 256). There was actually some weakening of the dollar in the months preceding the Plaza Hotel Agreement.

6. Canada, which had created an Economic Council of Canada in the early 1960s, modeled after our Council of Economic Advisers, actually abolished its body in 1991–1992. See *Economic Reform* (January 1994): 1.

7. At this point, a prominent econometrician (possibly Larry Chimerine of Chase according to a personal communication from Robert L. Bartley), branded Reagan as a "dunce" for saying that a trade deficit can sometimes be a sign of a healthy economy. See Robert L. Bartley, *Seven Fat Years*, p. 89.

8. Thatcher selected Alan Walters from Johns Hopkins, whose interesting autobiography appears in the *American Economist* (Fall 1989). This article would eventually create friction between Walters and Margaret Thatcher.

9. At the Hofstra Reagan Presidential Conference in 1993, I asked Kenneth Adelman whether Reagan was serious in his offer to give the Russians the results of a successful Strategic Defense Initiative. He assured me that this was one of four positions that he never could convince Reagan to abandon.

10. See Martin Walker, *Cold War*, p. 215.

11. The Soviets ostensibly wanted the unification and neutralization of Germany in the postwar years, whereas the United States initiated all of the acts that eventually divided Germany and rearmed the Federal Republic of Germany within NATO. It is perhaps significant that the creation of the Federal Republic of Germany preceded the birth of the German Democratic Republic, the issuance of the Westmark preceded the Eastmark, and the Warsaw Pact was announced after the creation of NATO. As late as the early 1950s, Kurt Schumacher, the West German Social Democrat, "wanted a united Germany, and believed that his could be made acceptable to the Soviets if all foreign troops were withdrawn and Germany became formally neutral. This was not an outlandish proposition." See Martin Walker, *Cold War*, p. 9.

12. *The Economic Report of the President, 1992*, p. 123. The Gini coefficient is a measure of the deviation of the income distribution from complete equality. It is the area between the diagonal depicting complete equality of the income distribution and the Lorenz curve as a percentage of the entire area of the triangle. A Gini coefficient of zero represents complete equality and a Gini of 1 would represent complete inequality.

13. Alan Greenspan, in testimony before the House Banking Committee, admitted that the trend toward increasingly unequal distribution of income is continuing and could be a major threat to our society, but claimed that reversing it is beyond the power of the Fed. See "Greenspan Predicts Revival of Growth Without Any Acceleration of Inflation," *The Wall Street Journal*, 20 July 1995, p. 2.

14. See my letter in *The New York Times*, 10 June 1992.

CHAPTER 9

1. Milton Friedman, "Oodoov Economics," *The New York Times*, 1 February 1992, *Op. Ed.*

2. The Bush administration did encourage the Internal Revenue Service to reduce withholding taxes, and later Bush stepped up defense spending, including the sale of F-16s to Taiwan. But, in general, the measures taken to use the political business cycle were weak and any positive results were not generally known before the November elections.

3. *Economic Reform* (April 1992).

4. Leonard Silk, *The New York Times*, 22 March 1992, p. 4E.

CHAPTER 10

1. Defense Budget Project, "Analysis of the Fiscal Year 1994 Defense Budget Request," Pamphlet, 14 April 1993, p. 7.

2. Solow, in particular, was the object of Joan Robinson's criticism of Bastard Keynesianism. See Marjorie Turner, *Joan Robinson and the Americans* (Armonk, NY: M. E. Sharpe, 1989).

3. Robert W. Solow and James Tobin, "Down to the Wire On the Deficit," *The New York Times*, 26 May 1993, p. A27.

4. See Lewis B. Kaden, chairman, and Lee Smith, director of the commission and editor, *America's Dream, Rebuilding Economic Strength* (Armonk, NY: M. E. Sharpe, 1992).

5. Senators Paul Sarbanes and Donald Riegle held hearings shortly after Christmas 1992 at which both Paul Samuelson and Paul McCracken were highly critical of Alan Greenspan's continued high real interest rates and generally tight monetary policy. Sarbanes would have liked to remove five representatives of the regional Federal Reserve Banks from the voting members on the open market committee since they do not require congressional approval.

6. For a clear exposition of the administration's response to Perot, see Don E. Newquist, "Perot Is Dead Wrong on NAFTA," *The New York Times*, *Op-Ed*, 10 May 1993, p. A-19. The author is chairman of the United States International Trade Commission.

7. See Kenneth S. Davis, *FDR into the Storm. A History* (New York: Random House, 1993, p. 389).

8. Martin Anderson, *Revolution*, p. 269.

9. Roosevelt was interested in "reflating" the economy as a result of pressure from agricultural interests, which explains his increasing the price of gold from $20.67 to $35 per ounce in several "illegal steps." The $35 per ounce price was confirmed by Congress in the Gold Reserve Act of January 1934. The whole procedure resulted in the "resignation" of Dean Acheson, who was acting head of the Treasury at the time. See my "Illegal Acts in Roosevelt's Bedroom?" *Economic Reform* (July 1995): 7. Although the general price level began to rise thereafter, the increase

in the price of gold was probably less important in reflating the economy than the public works program.

10. Kenneth S. Davis, *FDR*, p. 534. The Federal Reserve Board index of industrial production fell from 128 in December 1939 to 105 in March 1940. Unemployment in 1940 was above 10 million persons, a million more than in 1937.

11. Norton Grubb and Robert H. Wilson, "Trends in Wage and Salary Inequality, 1967–88," *Monthly Labor Review* (June 1992): 23–27. According to their conclusions, "During the 1967–88 period, wages and salaries became more unequally distributed with two spurts of increased inequality (1967–72 and 1980–86), and a period of relative stability (with some cyclical variation) during the peak of the Vietnam War." This increased inequality in the late 1960s is further evidence of an underheated economy at that time.

12. This view is in contrast to those of Michael Tugan-Baranowsky, a Ukrainian revisionist Marxist in the early twentieth century, who denied the interdependence of production and consumption. According to Tugan-Baranowsky, production could expand indefinitely without regard to the level or trend in consumption. Thus, the realization problem was a myth. See Paul Sweezy, *The Theory of Capitalist Development* (New York: Oxford, pp. 150 et seq.).

13. According to Marriner Eccles, "The popular analogy between the debt of an individual and the debt of a nation (an analogy Roosevelt had repeatedly used in public speech) is false." See Kenneth S. Davis, *The New Deal Years, 1933–37* (New York: Random House, 1979, p. 664). The chief exponent of balanced budgets by this time was the secretary of the treasury, Henry Morgenthau. Eccles, as chairman of the Federal Reserve Board of Governors, had doubled reserve requirements in the year before the Roosevelt recession, and was apparently trying to make amends.

14. Alvin H. Hansen, *The Dollar and the International Monetary System* (New York: McGraw-Hill, 1965, p. 152). At the Bretton Woods Conference these same ideas would be rejected by U.S. negotiators, particularly Edward Bernstein. The IMF's original charter did include a "scarce currency" clause designed to encourage symmetry of adjustment by placing pressures on chronically surplus countries to bring their surpluses down. According to Frances Stewart, *"Back To Keynesianism,"* p. 472, this clause has never been invoked.

15. An exception was the USSR from 1947 to 1954, when a disinflationary policy was pursued successfully by Stalin, producing positive real interest rates, in contrast to the negative real interest rates in the United States.

16. Alvin H. Hansen, *The Dollar*, p. 160.

17. See my review of David Marsh's *The Most Powerful Bank* in *Economic Reform* (March and April 1994).

CHAPTER 11

1. Japan, like the United States, has also moved in the opposite direction from that recommended by Keynes. Interest income received by individuals rose from 1.4 percent of national income in 1951 to 7.8 percent in 1974. See Shigeto Tsuru, *Japan's Capitalism: Creative Defeat and Beyond* (Cambridge, UK: Cambridge University Press, 1993, p. 111).

2. For a demystification of this organization, see Henry H. Schloss, *The Bank for International Settlements* (New York Graduate School of Business, *The Bulletin*, Nos. 65–66, September, 1970). In the United States, Jude Wannisky, Alan Greenspan, Jack Kemp, and Judy Shelton have at times been proponents of gold-based monetary policies.

3. See my *State and Discrimination*, p. 57.

4. For a good summary of the results, see Timothy A. Canova, "The Swedish Model Betrayed," *Challenge* (May–June, 1994): 36–40.

5. A Paasche index, such as the one adopted by France in the 1960s, would show less inflation since it is weighted according to a recent structure of consumption or market basket.

6. See my letter to *Business Week*, 31 May 1993, p. 18. Researchers at the Bureau of Labor Statistics estimate that the upward bias in the Consumer Price Index has been amounting to .6 of a percentage point. See Robert D. Hershey, Jr., "An Inflation Index Is Said to Overstate the Case," *The New York Times*, 11 January 1994, p. D-2. Even Alan Greenspan, in testimony before Congress, admitted in early 1994 that according to the Federal Reserve Board's own index, the true rate of inflation was between 1 percent and 2 percent, rather than the official 3 percent. He offered this suggestion to reduce the automatic increases in Social Security payments tied to the CPI, and thereby reduce the budget deficit.

7. According to Robert Skidelsky, *John Maynard Keynes*, Vol. II, p. 609, Keynes "would not have regarded armaments expenditures as a rational means of keeping the world booming. For Keynes, quantity of demand always had reference to quality of life. To cite the huge numbers of people, television sets, drugs, armaments as proof that mankind was solving its economic problems would have struck him as bizarre."

8. Albert T. Sommers, *The U.S. Economy Demystified* (Lexington, MA: Lexington Books, 1985, p. 117).

9. An early recognition of this phenomenon is found in the writings of Sir Roy Harrod, Keynes's first biographer and foremost disciple. In early June 1969, Harrod recognized that raising taxes, high interest rates, and "damping demand" are all inflationary. See A.L.K. Acheson *et al.*, eds., *Bretton Woods Revisited* (Toronto: University of Toronto Press, 1972, p. 15). See also Harrod's letter to *The New York Times*, 22 July 1969, in which he recognized that inflation was being sustained at too high a level by the Fed's restrictive policy—at a higher level than it would have been in the absence of a restricted Fed policy. The "cure" for demand-pull inflation, according to Harrod, was supply-side inflation, and vice versa. Any thought of zero inflation was furthest from his mind. In a letter to the *Economist* (July 29, 2969), Harrod wrote: "For some weeks now I have been uneasy about the economics implicit in our public policy: a few weeks ago I had a *conceptual breakthrough* [emphasis added]. A sharp distinction should be drawn between the effect on the general price level of a decline in aggregate demand, including its reduction by monetary and fiscal policies, when initially it is running above the supply potential of the economy, and the effect of a decline of aggregate demand when it is below the supply potential. . . . When aggregate demand is below the supply potential a reduction of demand will raise real unit costs . . . and therefore have a price-inflationary tendency . . . . If restrictive policy raises interest rates, this will tend to raise money costs of production. So will an increase of indirect

taxes and probably, also, to some extent, of direct taxes. . . . Most textbooks . . . are in need of revision." In Canada, this came to be known as the "Harrod Effect," or the "Harrod Dichotomy." See William Krehm, *Price in a Mixed Economy* (Thornwood Publications, Toronto, 1975) and John Hotson, "Comparative Static Analysis of Harrod's Dichotomy" (*Kyklos*, No. 2 [1972], pp. 154–66).

10. Sir Roy Harrod was particularly critical of Keynes's restoration of mercantilist respectability. Keynes recognized that his position was second best, but justified it by the depth of the Great Depression. See Joan Robinson, *The New Mercantilism* (Cambridge: Cambridge University Press, 1966, p. 3).

11. See my "Political Economy of Reparations," p. 125. India, Laos, and Cambodia forfeited reparations. Negotiations with Burma, the Philippines, Indonesia, and Vietnam (under Bao-Dai's rule) went on until as late as 1958, the total obligations for Japan coming to $1.012 billion, down from a requested total of over $20 billion, according to a personal communication from Shigeto Tsuru dated 24 August 1993.

12. See John Fialka, "U.S. Aid to Russia is Quite a Windfall—for U.S. Consultants," *The Wall Street Journal*, 24 February 1994, p. 1.

13. Estimates of the total amount of the subsidy vary from $.2 to $.9 billion per year. See Jonathan Eaton, "Credit Policy and International Competition," in Paul R. Krugman, ed., *Strategic Trade Policy and the New International Economics* (Cambridge, MA: The MIT Press, 1988, p. 117). Milton Friedman has still not given up on getting rid of this subsidy to exporters. See his "Budget Cutting: A Lot of Gain, Little Pain," *The Wall Street Journal*, 15 June 1995, p. A-14.

14. The original purpose of the Export-Import Bank was to finance exports to the USSR in 1934 after the Roosevelt administration belatedly recognized the Soviet Union. After World War II, the bank was made a wholly owned U.S. government corporation by the Export-Import Bank Act of 1945, providing for a banking corporation of the District of Columbia. It was used to lend to unstable countries threatened by local communists in the early postwar years. As late as 1950, the Ex-Im Bank granted such a loan of $100 million to Indonesia. See Melvyn P. Leffler, *A Preponderance of Power* (New York: W. W. Norton, 1994, p. 123).

15. Paul Krugman, *Peddling Prosperity* (New York: W. W. Norton, 1994, p. 123).

16. See Stephen D. Oliner and William L. Wascher, "Is a Productivity Revolution Under Way in the United States?" *Challenge* (November/December 1995): 19.

17. Myron Magnet, "The Truth About the American Worker," *Fortune*, 4 May 1992, 48–65. See also Paul Krugman, "Competitiveness: A Dangerous Obsession," *Foreign Affairs* (March/April 1994): 2844.

CHAPTER 12

1. Paul Volcker and Toyoo Gyohten, *Changing Fortunes* (New York: Times Books, 1992, pp. 168–181). Volcker had already been appointed to become Chairman of the Fed but he left his predecessor, William Miller, in Yugoslavia to give the Plenum defense of U.S. policy. See Robert L. Bartley, *Seven Fat Years*, p. 84, in which he claims that the U.S. delegation was also lectured enroute to Belgrade in Bonn.

2. Sidney Homer and Richard Sylla, *A History of Interest Rates* (New Brunswick, NJ: Rutgers University Press, 3rd ed., 1991, p. 430). Richard Sylla, who took over the

revision after the death of Homer, mentions that the third edition is the first one to even deal with real interest rates.

3. See footnote 13 in Chapter 8.

4. Robert L. Bartley, *Seven Fat Years*, p. 222, traces the bailout of the Farm Credit System in 1987 to farm expansion in the 1970s. See also Robert Guttmann, *How Credit-Money Shapes the Economy* (Armonk, New York: M. E. Sharpe, 1994), p. 239.

5. See *Business Week*, 10 May 1993, 83–84, and my letter in the 31 May issue, p. 18.

6. In my view, the Social Security tax is highly regressive and we would be better off financing such expenditures out of general revenues. When this policy was suggested by Governor Jerry Brown, Senator Moynihan claimed that this would mean the end of the program. In view of the highly effective lobby of senior citizens (AARP), this seems highly questionable.

7. August Heckscher, *Woodrow Wilson* (New York: Charles Scribner's Sons, 1991, p. 318).

8. On the surface, the "little Tigers" of Asia (South Korea, Taiwan, Hong Kong, Malaysia, Singapore, and Indonesia) seem to be an exception. Operating with under-valued currencies, they have used their export sectors to propel their economies forward—although South Korea typically runs an overall import surplus. This solution is relatively limited in the long run by the inability of other countries (with the exception of the rapidly growing economy of the Big Tiger, the People's Republic of China) to absorb their surpluses. The South Korean economy has already slowed down, which accelerated its recognition of the People's Republic of China, much to the displeasure of Taiwan. However, the latter is now having indirect relations with the Mainland through Hong Kong. Can the development of Greater China be far behind?

9. See my "From Reichbank to Bundesbank: Continuity or Change?" *Economic Reform* (March 1994): 7 and (April 1994): 4.

10. See Gerlinde Sinn and Hans-Werner Sinn, *Jumpstart, The Economic Unification of Germany* (Cambridge, MA: The MIT Press, 1992, p. 45).

11. Jane Perlez, "Western Banks To Relieve 40 Percent of Polish Debt," *The New York Times*, 12 March 1994, p. 1. In addition, Bulgaria received a 50 percent reduction in its outstanding debt. Under the so-called Brady Plan, Latin American countries have received an average of 33 percent debt reduction.

APPENDIX A

1. According to Barkley Rosser, in a letter dated 4 September 1995, the first use of the term "macroeconomics" was by Lawrence R. Klein, "Macroeconomics and Theory of Rational Behavior," *Econometrica*, April 1946, Vol. 14, pp. 93–108.

2. This essay, in slightly different form, originally appeared as the introduction to *The Search for Economics as a Science: An Annotated Bibliography*, copyright © by The Editors of Salem Press, Inc., and co-published by The Scarecrow Press, Inc., and Salem Press.

APPENDIX B

1. *The New York Times*, 31 May 1993, p. 38.

APPENDIX C

1. In this connection see Arthur Neff, "Unit Labor Costs in Eleven Countries," *Monthly Labor Review*, August, 1971, pp. 3–12. For the 1960s, unit labor costs rose roughly 20 percent for the U.S. manufacturers, compared with nearly 40 percent for manufacturers in other countries.

APPENDIX D

1. This is not meant to imply that there is any lack of repressed inflation in the Soviet-type system, but rather that the "repression" has gradually lessened over time.

2. At one point, the five-year moving average produced a growth in labor productivity of 3.8 percent, but the allowable wage increase remained unchanged. Thus, even if the price level had miraculously remained unchanged, the share of the pie going to labor would have declined.

3. During the period of the Kennedy guidelines, the wage increases for unorganized labor actually rose at a faster rate than those for organized labor, thus indicating the "effectiveness" of the guidelines. Another measure of the impact of the guidelines consists of the "Perry residuals." In this connection, see Paul Samuelson's comments in: The Industrial Council for Social and Economic Studies, *On Incomes Policy* (papers and proceedings of a conference in honor of Erik Lundberg), Stockholm, 1969, pp. 60 *et seq.*).

4. It may seem paradoxical to find a Republican administration being fairer to labor than the previous Democratic administration. The explanation of this phenomenon lies in the fact that the Democratic Party developed a reputation for being unfair to business during the New Deal years and has been forced in subsequent years to bend over backward to overcome this handicap. Thus, profits tend to be higher and antitrust prosecutions less troublesome under a Democratic administration.

5. These are the preliminary findings of Professor John W. Kendrick.

6. For a contrast between the present "recovery" and previous postwar recoveries, see Alfred Malabre's "The Outlook," *The Wall Street Journal*, 22 November 1971, p. 1. Exactly one year after the end of the recession (as designated by the NBER), the unemployment rate was higher than it was at an earlier date. Likewise, the underutilization of capital also increased. See *The Wall Street Journal*, 3 January 1972, p. 1.

7. The preceding remarks are based on a talk given at the California State University, San Jose, "Teach-In" on 3 November 1971.

APPENDIX E

1. Robert Skidelsky, *The Road from Serfdom* (New York: Viking Penguin, 1996, p. 83).

2. Robert M. Campbell, *Grand Illusions: The Politics of the Keynesian Experience in Canada 1945–1975* (Peterborough, Ont.: Broadview Press, 1987, p. 38).

3. *Economic Reform*, January 1994, p. 1.

4. Robert M. Campbell, *Grand Illusions*, p. 149.

5. David A. Wolfe, "The Rise and Demise of the Keynesian Era in Canada: Economic Policy, 1930–1982," in *Modern Canada 1930s–1980s, Readings in Canadian Social History*, ed. Michael S. Cross and Gregory S. Kealey (Toronto: McClelland & Stewart, 1984, p. 52).

6. Judy Shelton, *Money Meltdown* (New York: The Free Press, 1994, p. 29).

7. Dominion Bureau of Statistics, *Canada Year Book, 1961*, Ottawa, 1961.

8. For recent evidence of the operation of this "law," see Gillian Tett et al., "When Strength Is a Weakness," *Financial Times*, 9 August 1995, p. 9. The chronic weakness of the Italian lira combined with their relatively good economic growth is another example. I first used this term in my classes after Nixon's devaluation in 1971.

9. For a detailed account of this change in policy, see Thomas L. Towrie, "Crisis in Canada's Economy," *Challenge* (November 1962): 22–25.

10. Robert M. Campbell, *Grand Illusions*, p. 130.

11. Benjamin Higgins, *Economic Development* (New York: W. W. Norton, 1968, p. 596).

12. Pierre Elliott Trudeau, *Memoirs* (Toronto: McClelland & Stewart, p. 196).

13. See Linda McQuaig, *Beyond Closed Doors* (Markham, Ont.: Viking, 1987), especially Chapter 11, "Deficit Mania: How Ottawa Raised Taxes for Everyone But the Rich."

14. See editorial, "A Trial Balloon to Shoot Down," *Economic Reform* (August 1995): 1.

15. See *Economic Reform* (April 1992). According to a Canadian calculation, the Canadian real interest rate in 1990 was 10.9 percent compared to 4.7 percent in the United States and 5.1 percent in both Japan and the Federal Republic of Germany.

16. Robert Skidelsky, *The World After Communism*, p. 73. Skidelsky erroneously assumes that Keynesian economics didn't get started in the United States until the 1960s. Actually, it got started immediately after World War II with the creation of the Council of Economic Advisers, eventually headed by Leon Keyserling. By 1949 Keyserling was advocating a three-fold increase in government nonmilitary spending to get the U.S. economy out of the Truman recession of 1949. Eventually Paul Nitze took up his Keynesian ideas but substituted military for nonmilitary spending. Keyserling went along with this substitution and thereafter never saw an increase in military spending he didn't like. In my view, he is the classic "guns and butter" economist, or Military Keynesian. Although he maintained that he was not a "Keynesian," but rather a "pragmatist," this is a reflection of his idiosyncracies, which included a refusal to go along with the Treasury Accord of March 1951.

Annotated Bibliography

Acheson, A. L. K., Chant, J. F., and Prachowny, M. F. J., eds. *Bretton Woods Revisited*. Toronto: University of Toronto Press, 1972. Contains an important article by Sir Roy Harrod showing evidence of tradeoff between demand-pull and cost-push inflation.

Anderson, Martin. *Revolution*. New York: Harcourt Brace Jovanovich, 1988. An early supply-sider and executive secretary of PEPAB during the Reagan years, later he was instrumental in arranging the rebirth of PEPAB after its scuttling by Donald Regan.

Bartley, Robert L. *The Seven Fat Years, and How to Do it Again*. New York: The Free Press, 1992. A good history of the development of supply-side economics by a proponent, an editor of *The Wall Street Journal*.

Blinder, Alan S. *Hard Heads, Soft Hearts*. New York: Addison-Wesley, 1987. An early critique of monetarism and support for Keynesianism by the deputy chairman of the Federal Reserve Board in the Clinton years until 1996.

Bretton Woods Commission. *Bretton Woods: Looking to the Future*. A report (July 1994) of a commission headed by Paul Volcker recommending a return to fixed rates of exchange with wider bands than previously.

Burns, Arthur E. *Reflections of an Economic Policy Maker*. Washington, D.C.: American Enterprise Institute, 1978. Some writings of the important economic adviser to Presidents Eisenhower, Nixon, Ford, and Reagan. Includes Pepperdine College speech in which Burns recognizes the underheated economy during the Vietnam War.

Campbell, Robert M. *Grand Illusions: The Politics of the Keynesian Experience in Canada, 1945–1975*. Peterborough, Ontario: Broadview Press, 1987. Documents the Commercial Keynesianism of Canada as opposed to the Military Keynesianism of the United States.

Clarke, Peter. *The Keynesian Revolution in the Making, 1924–1936.* Oxford: Clarendon Press, 1988. Documents the conversion in March 1932 of Keynes's ideas on the relative importance of savings and investment. Henceforth, an active investment would outweigh passive savings.

Colander, David. "Was Keynes a Keynesian or a Lernerian?" *Journal of Economic Literature* (December 1984). An account of a high-level meeting between Lerner and Keynes at which Keynes admitted that functional finance was a logical extension of Keynesian ideas.

Colander, David C., and Harry Landreth, eds. *The Coming of Keynesianism to America.* Brookfield, UK: Edward Elgar, 1996. Interviews with early disciples of Keynesian economics: Bryce, Tarshis, Sweezy, Lerner, Hansen, Salant, Galbraith, Samuelson, Domar, Musgrave, Scitovsky, and Keyserling.

Congdon, Tim. *The Debt Threat.* London: Basil Blackwell, 1988. An indictment of high real interest rates by an economist familiar wih British financial circles.

Davis, Kenneth S. *FDR into the Storm. A History.* New York: Random House, 1993. A good documentation of the non-Keynesian economic policy of the New Deal and a recognition that the Roosevelt recession resulted from the balanced budget fetish of the time.

Dulles, John Foster. "The Reparations Problem." *Economic Journal* (June 1921): 186. An insightful understanding of the difficulties involved in the United States absorbing repayment for the loans to Great Britain and France during World War I.

Eatwell, John, ed. *The New Palgrave,* 1987. The four-volume economics encyclopedia available in most academic libraries.

———. *Whatever Happened to Britain.* London: Duckworth, 1981. A Keynesian analysis of the British economic dilemma at the beginning of the Thatcher years by the foremost adviser to the British Labour Party.

Eisner, Robert. *How Real Is the Federal Deficit?* New York: The Free Press, 1986. The best antidote for anyone worrying about the budget deficit, by a former president of the American Economic Association.

Frumkin, Norman. *Tracking America's Economy.* Armonk, NY: M. E. Sharpe, 1987. A guide to U.S. economic statistics.

Galbraith, Kenneth. *The Affluent Society.* New York: Houghton Mifflin, 1958. A pathbreaking break with his earlier *American Capitalism,* by the foremost U.S. institutionalist. Galbraith deplores private affluence and public squalor, the opposite of the conventional wisdom of the time, as well as today. An early opponent of Commercial Keynesianism, he was appointed to become ambassador to India to remove him from domestic policy discussions of the Kennedy administration.

———. *A Journey Through Economic Time.* New York: Houghton Mifflin, 1994. Interesting reminiscences by Galbraith of his role as an activist in government policymaking. Here he classifies President Reagan as a "Keynesian."

Gilder, George. *Wealth and Poverty.* New York: Basic Books, 1981. This book supposedly influenced Ronald Reagan to run on a supply-side economics program based on Kemp-Roth thinking in the Carter years. Calling for three successive 10 percent cuts in income tax rates, it would supposedly raise revenues to balance the budget by 1984. Since saving was now needed as a precondition of investment, Gilder called for an increase in the inequality of the income distribution to facilitate the creation of the required saving.

Greider, William. *Secrets of the Temple.* New York: Simon & Schuster, 1987. A definitive history of the Federal Reserve System, including Paul Volcker's misleading adoption of monetarism to disguise the sudden increase in real interest rates to "bite the bullet," as advocated by Milton Friedman and the Bundesbank.

Guttmann, Robert. *How Credit-Money Shapes the Economy: The United States in a Global System.* Armonk, NY: M. E. Sharpe, 1994. A pathbreaking critique of contemporary international monetary policy building on the works of John Maynard Keynes and Karl Marx. Guttmann criticizes the monetarist biases of the Maastricht Treaty, especially the early deregulation of capital movements within the European Economic Community. Guttmann develops a plan for a truly supranational form of credit-money (SNCM), building on Keynes's Bancor Plan. Under his plan, there would be no need for nations such as the United States benefiting from seigniorage. Neither would there be any need for the United States to import capital, especially from the poorest nations. Likewise, foreign aid and the writing off of foreign debt both become unnecessary with the ending of the Cold War.

Hansen, Alvin. *Fiscal Policy and Business Cycles.* New York: W. W. Norton, 1941. A persistent theme of Hansen, originating in his famous Harvard seminar in the late 1930s, was that unemployment was caused by a failure of private investment to match the level of saving at full employment income. With the effectiveness of monetary policy reduced by inelasticity, and high liquidity preference in a sluggish economy, the required level of aggregate demand would have to be provided by fiscal expenditures, responded to in the private sector by a multiplier-accelerator process. Drawing on his 1937 presidential address to the American Economic Association, Hansen placed the Keynesian model in a historic perspective and originated the secular stagnation thesis.

———. *The Dollar and the International Monetary System.* New York: McGraw-Hill, 1965. Emphasizes the point of Keynes at Bretton Woods that pressure on creditor countries to revalue their currencies is needed.

Harrod, Roy F. *Towards a Dynamic Economics.* London: Macmillan & Co., 1948. Calls for the elimination of a real interest rate to satisfy the socialist critics of capitalism.

Heckscher, August. *Woodrow Wilson.* New York: Charles Scribner's, 1991. Explains the origins of the Federal Reserve System.

Heilbroner, Robert. *The Debt and the Deficit.* New York: W. W. Norton, 1989. A popular demystification of the national debt and deficit-financing, including the recommendation that separate capital accounts be kept to measure public investment.

Heller, Walter. *Economics in the Public Service* (Papers in Honor of Walter W. Heller). Joseph Pechman and N. J. Simler, eds. New York: W. W. Norton, 1982. Tributes to the father of the "New Economics" of the Kennedy years.

——. *The Economy, Old Myths and New Realities*. New York: W. W. Norton, 1976. An interesting attempt to explain the difficulties experienced by the Bastard Keynesians at the time of crisis in their thinking.

——. *New Dimensions of Political Economy*. Cambridge, MA: Harvard University Press, 1966. Contains material presented in the Godkin lectures at Harvard. Here he reveals his own plans for revenue sharing that were eventually enacted during the Nixon administration. Heller celebrates the virtues of fiscal policy, the triumph of Keynesian thinking in the New Economics of the early 1960s, and the advent of modern welfare capitalism. He also talks about the important problems of educating politicians. Based on Heller's experience as chairman of the Council of Economic Advisers in the Kennedy administration.

Hession, Charles. *John Maynard Keynes: A Personal Biography of the Man Who Revolutionized Capitalism and the Way We Live*. London: Macmillan, 1983. An attempt to explain Keynes's genius on the basis of his sexual persuasion.

Homer, Sidney, and Richard Sylla. *A History of Interest Rates*. New Brunswick, NJ: Rutgers University Press, 3rd ed., 1991. A definitive source of interest rate statistics, including real interest rates for the first time in this latest edition.

Kaden, Lewis B., et al. *America's Dream, Rebuilding Economic Strength*. Armonk, NY: M. E. Sharpe, 1992. The report of the Cuomo Commission, resulting from the work of Laura Tyson and Lawrence Klein.

Kalecki, Michal. *Studies in the Theory of Business Cycles, 1933–39*. Introduction by Joan Robinson. New York: A. M. Kelly, 1966. Contains material first appearing in Polish and buttressing Robinson's claim that Kalecki was a forerunner of Keynes.

Kennan, George. "The Sources of Soviet Conduct." *Foreign Affairs* (July 1947): 566–82. The famous "Mr. X" article that outlined the U.S. containment policy of the USSR after World War II.

Keynes, John Maynard. *The Economic Consequences of the Peace*. London: Macmillan, 1919. A critical evaluation of the Versailles Treaty arguing that $30 billion worth of reparations by a truncated Germany was draconian and counterproductive.

——. *A Treatise on Money*. London: Macmillan, 1930. Milton Friedman's favorite book by Keynes; it was largely revised in the economics of the *General Theory*.

——. *General Theory of Employment, Interest and Money*. New York: Harcourt Brace, 1936. The pathbreaking book ushering in the Keynesian revolution.

——. *How to Pay for the War*. London: Macmillan, 1940. A reversal of gears to the *General Theory* on the appropriate economic policymaking for an overheated wartime economy. Robert Skidelsky argues that Keynes's proposals were libertarian and were approved by von Hayek.

Keyserling, Leon. *The Toll of Rising Interest Rates*. Washington, D.C.: Conference on Economic Progress, 1964. A plea for lower interest rates and criticizing the Kennedy economic policies from more of a classical Keynesian approach.

———. *"Liberal" and "Conservative" National Economic Policies and Their Consequences, 1919–1979*. Washington, D. C.: Conference on Economic Progress, 1979. A final pamphlet summarizing Keyserling's pragmatic approach to economic policy.

Klein, Lawrence. *The Keynesian Revolution*. New York: Macmillan, 1947. An early evaluation of the Keynesian revolution by the Nobel laureate econometrician.

Kolko, Gabriel. *Wealth and Poverty in America*. New York: Praeger, 1962. An economic historian challenges the conventional wisdom of the time that greater equality is being achieved in the advanced capitalist system.

Kornai, Janos. *The Socialist System: The Political Economy of Communism*. Princeton, NJ: Princeton University Press, 1992. The author, who divides his time between Budapest and Cambridge, is the foremost contemporary Hungarian economist, famous for his earlier work on *Anti-Equilibrium*. Here he presents a comprehensive critique of actually existing socialism.

Krehm, William. *Price in a Mixed Economy: Our Record of Disaster*. Toronto, Ont.: Thornwood Publications, 1975. Contains a discussion of the "Harrod dichotomy."

Krugman, Paul R., ed. *Strategic Trade Policy and the New International Economics*. Cambridge, MA: The MIT Press, 1988. The editor is the foremost critic of the international trade policy of the Clinton administration.

———. *The Age of Diminished Expectations and U.S. Economic Policy in the 1990s*, revised and updated ed. Cambridge, MA: The MIT Press, 1994. In the foreward, Paul Samuelson describes *The Age of Diminished Expectations* as a tour de force. In his view, Krugman is "the rising star of this century and the next." According to Krugman, the simple fact is that the U.S. economy is not doing well, compared with any previous expectation. Fortune magazine predicted in 1967 that real wages would increase by 150 percent by the year 2000. In fact real wages are no higher today than they were at the time of the earlier forecast and most likely considerably lower. In this short book, Krugman tries to explain why we are not making more of an effort to do something about our disappointing economy—which comes down in large part to the painfulness of the measures that we would have to take if we were serious about making a difference. The important things—those that affect the standard of living of larger numbers of people—are productivity, income distribution, and unemployment.

———. *Peddling Prosperity in the Age of Diminished Expectations*. New York: W. W. Norton, 1994. Krugman claims that no major U.S. economist became a supporter of supply-side economics. To reach this conclusion, he emphasizes Robert Mundell's eccentricities and overlooks Walter Heller, who finally admitted in the mid-1980s that he had been the first practicing supply-side economist, even though he didn't recognize the need for a new term to sell Commercial Keynesianism (Robert Lekachman's term in his *Age of Keynes* for Keynesians who are eager to cut taxes). Krugman is especially critical of the media pundits and, as a so-called New Keynesian, he presents insightful critiques of monetarism, rational expectations, and the New Classical schools.

————. "What Do Undergraduates Need to Know about Trade?" *American Economic Review* (May 1993): 23–26. A succinct critique of such pundits as Lester Thurow, Ira Magaziner, and Robert Reich, or what Krugman calls "pop internationalism." Students should regard trade as a production process that transforms exports into imports, and imports, not exports are the fruits of international trade. Krugman criticizes "job creation" as a result of NAFTA, and industrial policy generally.

Kuznets, Simon. *The Income Revolution*. New York: National Bureau of Economic Research, 1949. Claims that there is a movement toward greater equality in the income distribution in the advanced capitalist system and that this is dangerous since it reduces the savings available for investment. Although Kuznets was important in developing national income accounting in the 1930s at the National Bureau of Economic Research, he reflected the Bureau's anti-Keynesian bias.

Lekachman, Robert. *The Age of Keynes*. New York: Random House, 1966. An important popularizer of Keynes coins the term "Commercial Keynesianism" to describe some of the "New Economists." His *Greed Is Not Enough*, a critique of Reaganomics, seems not to recognize the similarities between supply-side economics and Commercial Keynesianism.

Lerner, Abba. *The Economics of Control, The Principles of Welfare Economics*, New York: Macmillan Co., 1944. Written during World War II, Lerner's idea of what principles should govern a socialist country, expanding on Oscar Lange's original book. His chapter on "Functional Finance" appeared in 1943 in *Social Research* and caused Keynes to regard Lerner as an impractical dreamer.

Malabre, Alfred L., Jr. *Lost Prophets*. Cambridge, MA: Harvard Business School Press, 1994. The well-known *Wall Street Journal* columnist second-guesses economic policymakers.

Mantoux, Etienne. *The Carthaginian Peace: or, The Economic Consequences of Mr. Keynes*. New York: Scribner's, 1952. A book by a French soldier, who died toward the end of World War II, rightly questioning the economics of Keynes in *The Economic Consequences of the Peace*, and contrasting it with the economics of the *General Theory*.

Marsh, David. *The Most Powerful Bank: Inside Germany's Bundesbank*. New York: Times Books, 1993. The *Financial Times* correspondent stresses the continuity of German bankers between Hitler and Adenauer, but ignores the differences in monetary policy in the two periods.

Martel, Leon. *Lend-Lease, Loans, and the Coming of the Cold War*. Boulder, CO: Westview Press, 1979. An investigation of the conflict between the State Department and the Treasury Department policies at the end of World War II, especially the Soviet request for a $1 billion loan that was mysteriously "lost" on some desk in the State Department.

May, Ernest R. *American Cold War Strategy: Interpreting NSC-68*. New York: St. Martin's, 1993. A reproduction of the formerly secret document and contemporary comments by some of the original actors, particularly Paul Nitze, who correctly gives credit to Leon Keyserling for the economics underlying the document.

Melamed, Leo, ed. *The Merits of Flexible Exchange Rates: An Anthology*. Fairfax, VA: George Mason University Press, 1988. Contains Milton Friedman's secret postelection message to Richard Nixon, urging the adoption of flexible exchange rates.

Menshikov, Stanislav. *Catastrophe or Catharsis? The Soviet Economy Today*. Moscow: Inter-Verso, 1991. A critical look at the transition to a postsocialist economy.

Miller, Nathan. *F.D.R.: An Intimate History*. New York: New American Library, 1983. An historian's analysis of the New Deal, including a misinterpretation of Keynes's ideas on monetary policy.

Moggridge, D. E. *John Maynard Keynes: An Economist's Biography*. London: Routledge, 1992. The definitive biography of Keynes from the standpoint of an economist, who also edited his *Collected Works*.

Nakamura, Takafusa. *Economic Growth in Prewar Japan*. New Haven: Yale University Press, 1983. Claims that the Japanese were the first practicing Keynesians.

Neikirk, William R. *Volcker, Portrait of The Money Man*. New York: Congdon & Weed, 1987. A good account of the work of the Volcker group working under Treasury Secretary John Connally, which eventually produced Nixon's New Economic Policy in 1971.

Nitze, Paul. *From Hiroshima to Glasnost*. New York: Grove Weidenfeld, 1989. Memoirs of a leading Cold Warrior.

Norton, Hugh S. *The Employment Act and the Council of Economic Advisers, 1946–1976*. Columbia, SC: University of South Carolina Press, 1977. A history of the first thirty years of the Council of Economic Advisers.

Nossal, Richard. *The Politics of Canadian Foreign Policy*. Scarborough, Ontario: Prentice-Hall, 1985. A good source of information on the Canadian foreign aid program.

Peterson, Wallace C. *Silent Depression: The Fate of the American Dream*. New York: W. W. Norton, 1994. A critical look at U.S. economy, but with little mention of monetary policy.

Polanyi, Michael. *Full Employment and Free Trade*. Cambridge: Cambridge University Press, 1948. A Keynesian view that with full employment there should be a flowering of free trade. Polanyi later become a follower of the Chicago School of Economics.

Prados, John. *Keeper of the Keys*. New York: William Morrow, 1991. A good account of the development of NSC-68, including the machinations of the politicians of that time.

Reston, James, Jr. *The Lone Star: The Life of John Connally*. New York: Harper & Row, 1989. Important information on the role of Connally in the development of the Nixon "shock."

Rima, Ingrid, ed. *The Joan Robinson Legacy*. Armonk, NY: M. E. Sharpe, 1991. An important collection of essays on Robinsonian economics.

Robinson, Joan. *Economics, An Awkward Corner*. New York: Pantheon, 1967. A short critique of the practice of Bastard Keynesianism and its results.

————. *The New Mercantilism* (Inaugural Lecture). Cambridge, U.K.: Cambridge University Press, 1966. An important Keynesian look at international trade.

Scheford, Bertram. "The General Theory for a Totalitarian State. A Note on Keynes's Preface to the German Edition." *Cambridge Journal of Economics* #4 (1980): 175–176. An investigation of the difference between the German version of the introduction and the one published in the *Collected Works*.

Schloss, Henry H. *The Bank for International Settlements*. New York: New York Graduate School of Business, *The Bulletin*, Nos. 65–66, September, 1970. One of the few published books on this important international organization, which most recently helped out in the Mexican peso crisis.

Schor, Juliet. *The Overworked American*. New York: Basic Books, 1991. Between 1969 and 1987, time on the job for the average American increased by 163 hours a year or by an extra month. Schor attributes this to the lower cost of management as a result of longer hours. Workers are also anxious to improve or maintain their living standard when real wages fall as they did. The consumerist treadmill and long-hour jobs have combined to form a cycle of work and spend.

Schultz, George. *Turmoil and Triumph*. New York: Charles Scribner's Sons, 1993. Memoirs of the former secretary of state in the Reagan years who played a major role in bringing about the surrender of the former Soviet Union.

Schultze, Charles. *Higher Oil Prices and the World Economy: The Adjustment Problem*. Washington, D.C.: Brookings Institution, 1975. An understanding of the OPEC price hike as similar to an increase in excise taxes imposed from abroad. As chairman of the CEA under Carter, he seemed to suffer from amnesia on this score.

Schumpeter, Joseph. *Capitalism, Socialism and Democracy*. New York: Harper & Row, 1942. Predicted that the victory of Keynesian economics would produce a slowdown in the growth of the advanced capitalist system. According to Schumpeter, the former volatility was a major source of dynamism.

Schweizer, Peter. *Victory, The Reagan Administration's Strategy That Hastened the Collapse of the Soviet Union*. New York: Atlantic Monthly Press, 1994. Claims that William Casey, head of the CIA, arranged with the Saudis to break out of the oil cartel's quota to bring down the price of oil and cut into foreign exchange earned by Soviet oil exports.

Scitovsky, Tibor. "Lerner's Contribution to Economics." *Journal of Economic Literature*, (December 1984): 1547–91. An appreciation of one of the foremost Keynesians, who added functional finance to the economics of the *General Theory*. See also his contributions to David Colander's *The Coming of Keynesianism to America*.

Shelton, Judy. *Money Meltdown, Restoring Order to the Global Currency System*. New York: The Free Press, 1994. A case for the return of the gold standard.

Skidelsky, Robert. *John Maynard Keynes*, Volume 2. London: Macmillan, 1992. A second of three promised volumes on the life and work of Keynes, by a historian.

———. *The Road from Serfdom*. New York: Viking-Penguin, 1996. A non-Sovietologist's look at the fall of communism.

Sobel, Robert. *The Worldly Economists*. New York: The Free Press, 1980. An interesting study of seven influential economic policy makers in the postwar years in the United States, including Leon Keyserling.

Solomon, Steven. *The Confidence Game*. New York: Simon & Schuster, 1995. The author traveled twice around the world interviewing central bankers and monetarists. His views generally reflect the monetarist viewpoint and show little evidence of his understanding of Keynes. See my review in *Economic Reform* (March 1996): 7. He does recognize the Keynesian tendencies of Reagan and the role of high real interest rates in increasing the inequality of the income distribution.

Stein, Herbert. *Presidential Economics*. Simon and Schuster, 1985. Memoirs of President Nixon's chairman of the Council of Economic Advisers.

Steindl, Josef. *Maturity and Stagnation in American Capitalism* (with a new introduction by the author). New York: Monthly Review Press, 1976. This book was originally published in 1952, when growth rather than stagnation was more obvious. It lays bare what Marx called capitalism's "laws of motion" and is recognized as one of the most original and important contributions to our study of monopoly capitalism. According to Steindl, the function of competition is the elimination or prevention of excess capacity, which leads to a lower rate of profit and a tendency toward stagnation. Oligopoly leads to an increase in profit margins and a fall in effective demand. His stagnation thesis has become more relevant since 1970.

Sweezy, Paul. *The Theory of Capitalist Development*. New York: Oxford, 1941. A definitive examination of the schools of Marxist thought on the eve of World War II. Written by the dean of U.S. Marxists, the author was also well schooled in modern academic economic theory at Harvard and the London School of Economics in the 1930s. This classic has not been challenged or even approached by any later study.

Talbot, Strobe. *The Master of the Game*. New York: Alfred A. Knopf, 1988. The author became an important decision-maker in the U.S. state department and an adviser on Russian affairs under President Clinton.

Temin, Peter. *Did Monetary Forces Cause the Great Depression?* New York: W. W. Norton, 1976. A rebuttal to Milton Friedman's view that poor monetary policy caused the Great Depression. Temin finds that a sharp drop in consumption preceded the Great Depression. There was a tendency for productive capacity to outrun effective demand as real wages increased more slowly than productivity in the 1920s.

———. *Lessons from the Great Depression*. Cambridge, MA: The MIT Press, 1989. In these three lectures delivered at Oxford, Temin looks at the international causes of the Great Depression, which affected all capitalist countries. The attempt to restore the international gold standard and the continuation of the deflationary thinking behind the gold standard are the prime suspects.

Trudeau, Pierre. *Memoirs*. Toronto: McClelland & Stewart, 1993. An account of Canada's economic problems in the 1970s by the world's foremost non-military leader of that time.

Tsuru, Shigeto. *Japan's Capitalism: Creative Defeat and Beyond.* Cambridge, UK: Cambridge University Press, 1993. A look at the recovery process in a totally defeated Japan after World War II. Tsuru emphasizes the active role of the Japanese government in encouraging the continuing success that followed. He analyzes the welfare significance of Japan's money-oriented affluence, and the emergence of a distinctive "corporate capitalism" based on an unbalanced expansion of the internal surplus in firms. He concludes that the successes have led to a new set of intractable problems.

———. *The Economic Development of Modern Japan: The Selected Essays of Shigeto Tsuru.* Vol. 2. Aldershot, UK: Edward Elgar, 1995. A collection of essays by Japan's foremost economist, including "Has Capitalism Changed?" which was published as a small book followed by comments by world-famous economists in 1961. Tsuru studied under Schumpeter at Harvard before World War II and is thoroughly at home in both Marxist and Keynesian paradigms.

Turgeon, Lynn. "The Enigma of Soviet Defense Expenditures." *The Journal of Conflict Resolution* (June 1964). Argues that "secrecy" was the Soviet Union's secret weapon in the 1950s, allowing them to economize on defense spending and achieve rapid growth in that decade. This advantage was later lost as a result of our "spies-in-the-sky."

———. "The Crisis in Post-Keynesian Economics." *Quarterly Review of Economics and Business* (December 1971). Argues that post-Keynesian analysis of Paul Samuelson was in crisis because of "stagflation." Based on lectures given in Prague and Budapest in the summer of 1970.

———. "Political Economy of Reparations." *New German Critique* (Winter 1973). Argues that reparations were a major factor that fueled the Cold War because of the different abilities of the USSR and the United States to absorb reparations.

———. *The Advanced Capitalist System.* Armonk, NY: M. E. Sharpe, 1980. Lectures on the U.S. economy delivered at Moscow State University in the fall of 1978, including questions by Soviet students.

———. "Last Call for Market Capitalism" (review article on George Gilder's *Wealth and Poverty*), (*Social Policy*, May/June 1981). Argues that Reaganomics can bring positive results in the short and medium run, but in the last analysis it is counterproductive in the long run.

———. *State and Discrimination.* Armonk, NY: M.E. Sharpe, 1989. A study of affirmative action programs in the former Soviet Union and the United States, arguing that the programs of the former influenced the latter. Now that the Cold War is over, U.S. affirmative action programs are apparently disposable.

Turner, Marjorie. *Joan Robinson and the Americans.* Armonk, NY: M. E. Sharpe, 1989. A preliminary biography of Robinson that will eventually be supplemented by the definitive Harcourt biography.

Varga, Eugene. "Reparations by Hitler's Germany and Its Accomplices." *Voina i rabochi klass* 10 (October 15, 1943). The economic case for Germany's reparations to the USSR by the world-famous Hungarian economist residing in Moscow.

Vatter, Harold G. *The U.S. Economy in the 1950s*. New York: W. W. Norton, 1963. The best history of the economics of the Eisenhower years.

Viner, Jacob. "German Reparations Once More." *Foreign Affairs* (July 1943). An attempt to rectify the reparations problem after World War II on the basis of the experience after World War I, using Keynesian principles.

Volcker, Paul, and Toyoo Gyohten. *Changing Fortunes*. New York: Times Books, 1992. Lectures at Princeton after Volcker stepped down from his job as chairman of the Federal Reserve Board in 1987.

Walker, Martin. *The Cold War: A History*. New York: Henry Holt, 1995. The Washington corresondent for the *Manchester Guardian* gives an insightful look at the fall of communism, discussing the role of NSC-68 and President Reagan's Keynesian program in bringing this about.

Wallace, Henry. *The Price of Vision, The Diary of Henry A. Wallace 1942–46*. New York: Houghton Mifflin, 1973. Memoirs of the vice president and former secretary of agriculture during World War II.

Wattel, Harold, ed. *The Policy Consequences of John Maynard Keynes*. Armonk, NY: M. E. Sharpe, 1985. Papers presented at a Keynes Conference at Hofstra University on the 100th anniversary of Keynes's birth in 1883.

Index

ABOUT THE AUTHOR

LYNN TURGEON is Professor Emeritus of Economics at Hofstra University. He is the author of *The Contrasting Economics* (1963 and 1969), *The Advanced Capitalist System* (1980), and *State and Discrimination* (1989).

ISBN 0-313-30024-0

HARDCOVER BAR CODE